I0765749

Butt Out.

A scientific approach to quit smoking.

Hemant Poudyal, Ph.D.

Butt out. A scientific approach to quit smoking.

Copyright © 2019 Hemant Poudyal

All rights reserved.

ISBN: 9781691917334

Published by Hemant Poudyal 2019

Kyoto, Japan

No parts of this publication may be reproduced, stored in a retrieval system, or transmitted in any form or by any means, electronic, mechanical, photocopying, recording, or otherwise, without the prior written permission of the copyright owner.

This book is sold subject to the condition that it shall not, by way of trade or otherwise, be lent, resold, hired out, or otherwise circulated without the publisher's prior consent in any form of binding or cover other than that in which it is published and without a similar condition including this condition being imposed on the subsequent purchaser. Under no circumstances may any part of this book be photocopied for resale.

TABLE OF CONTENTS

Disclosures and Fun Facts

I am not affiliated or have not received any funding, stipend, salary, or honorarium from the tobacco industry or any of its subsidiaries. I don't sell seminars, online courses, or run quit smoking "clinics." I don't have a website and, therefore, cannot ask you to go to my website for additional resources or worst, join my subscriber list so that I can spam you later. I am just an academic nerd who loves knowledge, gadgets, and the original trilogy of Star Wars.

More importantly, I believe that scientific information should be made accessible beyond the walls of university libraries or journal websites in a form that is relatively easy to understand and can be used to solve real-world problems. This book is the manifestation of this principle. All the information you need to quit smoking lies within this book. The only thing I demand is that you think about your smoking behavior critically and logically as you read.

Feel free to connect with me if you need additional assistance to quit smoking. Since you already pay me a good salary through taxes (I work for a public university), I will not charge you for the extra help if it can get you to quit smoking. Instead, I request that you help another smoker to quit smoking in exchange for my time. As I don't use any social media, the easiest way to connect with me is by email (scan the QR code on the following page). Also, let me know your experience using this book and how you progress as a nonsmoker.

As excited as I am to help a billion smokers escape from slavery to cigarettes, my time is mostly consumed by lectures, research, writing books, and parenthood. Since I intend to read and respond to all your emails personally, it will help my support staff and me a great deal if you include "Butt out." in the subject line of your email.

Connect with me by scanning this QR code.

Dedicate to 250,000,000 people already killed and a billion more who will die by the end of this century as a direct result of smoking.

The Three Nudges

*For the great doesn't happen through impulse alone,
and is a succession of little things that are brought
together ... And the great isn't something accidental; it
must be willed.*

-Vincent van Gogh, post-impressionist painter

It feels great to be free. Free after sixteen years of slavery to smoking. Free from constant coughing, wheezing, headaches, and lack of breath. Free from walking around with a pack of cigarettes (plus the lighter, portable ashtray, and mint-flavored gums) bulging from my pant pockets. Free from searching for designated smoking areas everywhere I went. Free from the awful metallic taste in my mouth that greeted me every morning. Free from the revolting smell of tobacco smoke emanating from my clothes and hair. But most importantly, free from the guilt of not giving my undivided attention to the people I love and the hobbies I enjoy. The feeling of finally becoming a nonsmoker [fn01] again is so liberating that it will be a crime against humanity if I do not share the knowledge—gained by being a smoker and a medical scientist—on how to permanently quit smoking.

[fn01] Recent converts to vegetarianism do not go around telling people that they are an ex-meat eater. Following the same logic, nonsmoker is the appropriate terminology to describe someone who has quit smoking than ex-smoker. The term ex-smoker implies that smoking is still a part of your identity. When you quit smoking, cigarettes cease to be anything but a minor footnote in your life; just like this one.

But like my mother says, never take candies and life advice from strangers. So, it essential that you, the readers, get to know me and my credentials before I show you how smoking has enslaved you and help you see the path towards becoming a permanent nonsmoker.

I received my doctorate from the University of Queensland, Australia. I specialize in the study of how food and tobacco cause heart disease and ways to prevent it. I have been working at Kyoto University, Japan, as a lecturer and researcher since 2014. I have published several original research articles in some of the top scientific journals and have authored four books.

I was also a smoker for sixteen years. I smoked my first cigarette at the age of fifteen, and the number of cigarettes per day peaked during my doctoral years. I was smoking over two packs a day and unable to afford cigarettes after a price hike, I started rolling my own cigarettes. I was taking smoking breaks so frequently at work that Prof. Lindsay Brown, my mentor and advisor for the doctoral dissertation, dropped subtle hints such as *"how can you smoke after knowing the risks of heart disease and cancer due to smoking?"* Although he made a valid point, I have learned more about smoking from being a smoker than a medical researcher.

After I finished my doctoral research and took up an independent research and teaching position at Kyoto University, the situational irony started to become embarrassing. I needed a cigarette before and after my conference presentations and lectures, which were mainly about heart disease and the dangers of junk diet and smoking. I still remember some of the bemused faces in the audience who had seen me outside the building, minutes before the lecture, puffing out silky white smoke.

Ashamed of my habit, I spend the last five years as a smoker trying to quit smoking. Those five years were riddled with countless failures. The failures, however, were not for nothing. My scientific training helped me dissect the failures, analyze them, and corroborate my experiences with the findings reported in the scientific literature. I tried to generalize my findings by roping in all my smoking buddies [fn02] to provide me with their experiences with smoking and failed quit attempts.

I focused on analyzing failed quit attempts because there was much to learn from the failures. If so many people around the world attempt to quit and fail each year, we must all be doing something wrong. Given the regularity at which smokers fail to quit smoking despite strong desire, there was a distinct possibility that we were all doing the *same* thing wrong. Or, the high failure rate could be because of nicotine addiction, as we all believe. Analyzing failed quit attempts helped me better understand why smokers fail so often.

I had two notable quit attempts in the last five years as a smoker when I was actively trying to quit smoking. The first one was in 2012. I quit smoking using directed hypnosis (listening to a recording of hypnotic instructions) and an additional session with a licensed hypnotherapist. I was smoke-free for about three months and then relapsed. I cannot remember the circumstances of this relapse, but I think it was at a party. Nevertheless, this attempt was notable because it was the first time since smoking the first cigarette that I had abstained for more than twenty-four hours.

The second notable attempt produced the most prolonged period of abstinence from smoking before I finally quit smoking for good. I quit for about nine months after reading *The EasyWay to Quit Smoking* by Allen Carr. Carr challenged everything I believed about smoking and showed how smokers are brainwashed into believing the lies about the benefits of smoking. But smokers tend to resist when presented with any information against smoking, and I was no different. I resisted and tried to find loopholes in the information presented in Carr's book. Not because I was critical about the book, but I desperately wanted Carr to be wrong so that I could justify smoking.

Unfortunately for me, I was successful and found two loopholes in Carr's arguments that I used to justify a relapse. I felt then as I feel now that the way Carr dealt with the issue of smoking as a classic case of the drug (nicotine) addiction was not well-founded. Also, I found his two core

---

fn02 Smoking buddies are people we call friends simply by virtue of spending some common time smoking and engaging in chit-chat at the same location. Although some smoking buddies go on to become lifelong friends, there is generally no emotional bonding, and they are casual acquaintances at best.

arguments that smoking is drug addiction, and nicotine has little or no withdrawal effects, conflicting. If nicotine is a drug that causes the addiction, then removal of the drug when one quits smoking should produce strong withdrawal effects, as is the case with classic drug addiction. We can also look at this in reverse. If the withdrawal symptoms of nicotine are weak or non-existent, as Carr claimed, perhaps nicotine is not as addictive as we have been led to believe. Only one of these situations can be real. Resolving this conundrum poised by Allen Carr's otherwise excellent book years later helped me quit smoking for good. I will discuss the evidence for nicotine addiction in the next chapter.

I tried hypnotherapy and reading Allen Carr's book several times after the first experience with each produced short periods of abstinence. They had worked once, and I hoped that they could get me to quit again. Unfortunately, taking up hypnotherapy and reading Allen Carr's book multiple times did not lead to another quit attempt. The fact that both methods worked only once suggests that it was the novelty of the technique that fueled the quit attempt.

Researchers have investigated both hypnotherapy and the EasyWay method as a tool that may aid quit smoking efforts. There is very little evidence to support the efficacy of hypnotherapy in quitting smoking [1]. Carr's method fares much better in comparison. About 20 percent of smokers remained quit after one year of attending EasyWay seminars or reading the book [2-4]. The quit rate with Carr's method is, of course, vastly lower than the 90 percent success rate at his clinics based on their money-back guarantee. Other studies have found that the abstinence produced by the EasyWay method is no better than that produced by chance alone despite participants having a strong motivation (all participants of this study had been recently diagnosed with head and neck cancer) and receiving the book for free [4].

Nevertheless, I must thank my hypnotherapist and Allen Carr for giving me a taste of liberation, albeit short-lived, from smoking cigarettes. I have also experimented with using nicotine patches, gums, and gradually cutting down the number of daily cigarettes. None of these methods resulted in abstinence over one day. I will deal with nicotine replacement therapy and the cigarette reduction method in later chapters.

I finally quit smoking about three years ago after our third miscarriage in 2016. Desperate to experience parenthood, my wife and I radically modified our lifestyles as this was the only known risk factor we could adjust. We made significant changes to our diets, took up exercise, and I quit smoking. We invited our beautiful daughter, Nimisha Sayuri, into our family about eighteen months ago.

I don't want you to think that the hypocrisy of being a smoker and a proponent of a healthy lifestyle or our recurrent miscarriages led me to quit smoking. If these motivations could get me to quit, I would have stopped smoking years ago, and certainly before my wife and I decided to become pregnant. I knew fully then that both maternal and paternal smoking increases the risk of congenital abnormalities and miscarriages. Exposing my never-smoker wife to secondhand tobacco smoke posed an additional threat. The first miscarriage should have been the kick up the backside that I needed to quit smoking, but it wasn't. Like a typical smoker, I naively believed that I was somehow immune to the devasting effects of smoking.

A valuable lesson I learned from my failed quit attempts and life circumstances was that motivation is an overrated concept. Motivation is the spark that leads to action. Motivation, however, does not produce action most of the time, and when it does, it does not help sustain the action. Everybody knows somebody who wants to hit the gym to reduce their body weight or high cholesterol but fails to ever step foot in one. Some are highly motivated, pay for annual membership to a popular gym, and only go for a few weeks. In the first scenario, there was motivation but no action, and in the second, there was action, but it was not sustained. Similarly, smokers fail to quit despite numerous motivations (health, money, etc.), and if they do quit, the motivations do not take them far, and many ultimately relapse.

Motivation translates into action only when we feel the chances of success are higher than failure. This is where determination comes into the picture. We all know determination as the *I-will-succeed-no-matter-what* attitude. This attitude can only develop after we learn to remove barriers so that we can prevail "no matter what" life throws at us. In a practical sense, building determination is, therefore, an act of logic and reasoning.

In the context of smoking, one may be motivated to quit smoking for health reasons, but how will the smoker deal with stress, parties, or withdrawal symptoms after quitting? A person determined to quit smoking will have the answer to this question. In my case, avoiding professional embarrassment and experiencing parenthood were significant motivations to quit smoking, but this was not enough to become a nonsmoker because I lacked determination.

I can trace back my determination to quit smoking to at least three nudges that brewed in my mind over time. I call these nudges because they were seemingly small events, but each snowballed into producing a huge impact. The first nudge was a casual but often repeated comment from my friend Dr. Zi Peng Li. Every time I told Li about making yet another attempt to quit smoking, he responded by paraphrasing Mark Twain: "*Quitting smoking seems easy. You do it all the time!*" This causal statement had a greater impact on me than Li intended.

At the time, I thought of the process of quitting as getting over a hump; once you smoke that final cigarette and promise never to smoke another one, that's it. I did not put any effort into maintaining my status as a nonsmoker. Li's wisdom changed my approach from *quitting-smoking-is-like-getting-over-a-hump* to *staying-quit-requires-effort*. When I started my final quit attempt, I took this quote from Li, added a sentence of my own, and displayed it prominently on my work desk, as my desktop background, and on my smartphone's lock screen. This simple act enabled me to focus on staying smoke-free instead of getting over the hump.

Quitting smoking is easy. I do it all the time.

But staying quit is hard.

One of my Japanese students provided the second nudge in 2014. At that time, I was focused on researching the impact of poor nutrition on diabetes, obesity, and heart disease. After one of my research presentations, a young student came up to me and asked if my research was relevant and urgent in the Japanese context? Unable to understand the intent of the question, I asked the student to elaborate. She said, "*there are more smokers in Japan who are at risk of heart disease, then there are obese and diabetic people.*"

I spend a few days looking up scientific publications on the changes in the number of smokers over the years and the deaths and disabilities caused by smoking. I will spare you the boring details, but what I had found was enough to provoke my scientific curiosity. I decided to expand the research interest of our group to include smoking as a risk factor of heart disease. This expansion of my research theme made smoking even more embarrassing for me. But this change was an opportunity to gain deep insights into the workings of the tobacco industry and the process of formulation of tobacco-related health policies. The lesson learned here was that our current public health policies against smoking were designed to fail, and I could see the flaws in the strategies both as a smoker and a medical researcher.

I was incredibly lucky with the third nudge. It was provided by a book that has nothing to do with smoking but dealt with psychology and economics. I sometimes regret choosing physiology as my specialty. If I had the DeLorean from the 1985 sci-fi classic "Back to the Future," I would travel back in time and tell my younger self to take up the study of human psychology [fn03]. Instead, I now read books and articles written by behavioral psychologists as my favorite pastime activity to make up for my losses. One such book that I read was *Thinking, Fast and Slow* by Nobel Prize-winning psychologist Daniel Kahneman. *Thinking, Fast and Slow* was instrumental in explaining why I participated in the highly illogical and irrational act of smoking and showing me how motivations for behavioral change work.

I will elaborately describe the insights from the three nudges in the subsequent chapters. Here, it will suffice to say that together, the three nudges helped me better understand the social and psychological factors that are always at work to derail any effort to quit smoking. The three nudges also produced an important change in my approach to quitting—the act of smoking the final cigarette was not enough, and more effort was needed to maintain your status of being a nonsmoker.

You now know a little bit about me and my motivations; let me tell you about what you will not be reading in this book.

This book does not contain a method to quit smoking. A method implies a set of step-by-step procedures that can produce reproducible results. No such thing exists or can exist to help you quit smoking. Every smoker is different. We all had unique circumstances and reasons that led us to take up smoking and have unique motivations to quit. The duration for which one has been smoking, local social norms, influences, and experiences in life all add to the complexity of the problem, ultimately making the one-shoe-fits-all approach of quit smoking unusable. Instead, I offer a more straightforward approach. I will help you understand the hows and whys of

---

[fn03] To answer the most common question I get when I make this statement in public: no, I will not try to stop my younger self from take up smoking in the first place if I can travel back in time. I know that I would have failed to convince the fifteen-year-old me. Read more about this in the chapter *The First Cigarette*.

your smoking behavior, and you will see the path, tailor-made for your circumstances, to become a nonsmoker.

While we are on the issue of what this book does not contain, I have superfluously dealt with the health impacts of smoking. Smokers know more about the disastrous health effects of smoking than expert researchers. Governmental and non-governmental efforts to inform the public on the harmful effects of smoking have worked very well in the sense that public perception is at an all-time high. But this scare campaign, which I prefer to call the doom and gloom campaign, has mostly failed to motivate smokers to quit smoking. I, for one, did not care much for the gory images on cigarette packs. For most smokers, the doom and gloom campaign and the resultant health scare when they later discover a lump under the jawbone have the opposite effect; the smoker's urge to smoke increases. As you will see in later chapters, one of the lessons from Kahneman beautifully explains why we immediately reach for a cigarette with every health scare.

Smoking causes 70 percent of all lung cancers. Pause here for a minute and think about how the previous statement that I presented so abruptly made you feel. Did your urge to smoke go up? Most likely, it did. But did this fact affect the resolve to quit smoking in any way? If health scares could get you to quit smoking, then there would be no need for this book; you would already be a happy nonsmoker. So, no easy quit methods or health scares in this book. Instead, I have presented arguments, supported by scientific evidence, to help you understand why you picked up the first cigarette, developed the habit, and how to find your way out of this slavery to cigarettes. I have divided the contents of this book into two parts.

In part one, I will dispel some myths about smoking. A popular myth in vogue is that nicotine is more addictive than cocaine and heroin. There is absolutely no scientific evidence to support these claims [5]. On the contrary, the current scientific evidence questions the addictiveness of nicotine [6]. As smokers, past or current, we do not need any scientific validation for the addictiveness of cigarettes. But is nicotine as addictive as we have been told? I will present the scientific evidence in the next chapter on nicotine addiction, and you can judge for yourself.

Please be highly critical about everything I say but importantly about everything you have come to believe about smoking. There is so much misinformation, particularly on health issues, that readers often find it challenging to comprehend conflicting reports. It is for this reason that the contents of this book draw heavily on scientific research of the past three decades, and I have supported all statements of fact with scientific evidence marked by the superscripted reference number at the end of the sentence [Like this]. You may look up the source of these arguments using the detailed bibliography at the end of the book. Although superscripted reference number at the end of the sentence may make the reading experience slightly less pleasant, I feel it is essential to prioritize credibility over convenience.

To fully understand your addiction to cigarettes, we need to travel back in time and understand the circumstances that led you to smoke the very first cigarettes. We will be taking this trip to the past in chapters *The First Cigarette* and *Brain-hijacking*. At the end of part one, you will have a thorough understanding of why you smoke and what smoking does for you.

In part two of this book, I will give you the six stages that smokers take to quit smoking. All those who have attempted to quit but failed, quit but relapsed, or have remained quit after years go through the same six stages of quitting smoking. So, what determines the success of a quit attempt if both successful and unsuccessful quitters are going through the same six stages? This will be our quest in the second part of this book. I will show you how successful quitters build determination to quit and create a quit smoking plan that greatly outlives the act of smoking the final cigarette. None of my arguments are based on whimsical thoughts or interviews with a handful of smokers whom you, the readers, have never met. Instead, I have cogently argued based on publicly available scientific evidence from medical and psychological research. In the second part, I will also exploit my past smoking experience to evaluate the scientific evidence both as a smoker and a researcher and present the evidence in a way that is relevant to the everyday smoker.

Needless to say, but I am going to say it anyway, I don't believe in magic and am highly skeptical of anything that even sounds like magic. If you were looking for a quick fix, I am sorry that I will have to disappoint you. I cannot promise that quitting smoking will be easy, effortless, or an overnight process where you suddenly wakeup a nonsmoker. But quitting does not have to be difficult either. Quitting smoking is possible if smokers receive and act on the nudges they receive. Just the way my friend Li, the young student, and Kahneman's book gave me the three nudges to build the determination to quit, I wish to give you your three nudges.

Like I said before, quitting smoking is an active process and needs deliberate effort from the smoker. Fortunately, the deliberate effort only involves three things: honest introspection, smoking mindfully, and taking baby steps. You must act on these three nudges as you read about them in the following paragraphs. They are essential, and nothing I say in the subsequent chapters will have any effect on your smoking behavior unless you act on these three nudges.

Honest introspection

Smoking makes otherwise honest people dishonest. If you think of it, smoking that very first cigarette years ago was a dishonest act. You probably took the first puffs in secrecy, and all subsequent cigarettes reinforced dishonesty to sustain the smoking habit. How many times have we slipped out of weddings, birthday parties, and corporate events to smoke a few quick puffs with the excuse of going to the bathroom? If you started smoking as a teenager, do you remember how you convinced your parents of your sainthood when they accused you of smoking? Do you use minty candies and gums to mask the filthy smell of cigarettes? I can go on, but I think you get the point.

What surprised me, when I made my final quit attempt, was how smoking also taught me to be dishonest to myself and live in denial. In the first few years after I became a regular smoker, I believed that I was not addicted and could quit whenever I wanted. Just a few years ago, I would swear with one hand on the Bible that smoking relieved my stress and helped me deal with my problems. During dire times, I believed that cigarette was a friend. These are the lies that keep us hooked to cigarettes.

Through honest introspection, I was able to see, beyond the lies and denials, that I picked up that first cigarette all those years ago because of poor self-esteem. I was fifteen years old then, and smoking was an easy way to look cool, sophisticated, wealthy, manly, and brave. Most smokers take up smoking because of these motivations, and the fact that we wanted to be more than who we were exposes the underlying role of self-esteem in smoking initiation. As I grew older, my self-esteem improved with experience. I certainly didn't have any self-esteem issues at the age of thirty-one when I quit smoking.

Honest introspections also helped me realize that cigarettes, if anything, destroyed my self-esteem. I was constantly lethargic, had shortness of breath, was overweight, was embarrassed about the reeking smell of tobacco on my clothes and hair, and generally believed that I was a weak-willed person. Amazingly, all of these problems, except being overweight, vanished immediately after quitting smoking. I appreciated these positive changes more because I had become fully aware of the damage smoking caused to my physical and mental wellbeing. I couldn't see before my final quit attempt that it wasn't the cigarette that improved my self-esteem; it was my life experiences.

Poor self-esteem was not the only reason I smoked. After months of lighting that first cigarette, smoking became an essential part of my support system for dealing with stress. I also believed that smoking helped me think clearly and creatively, both of which are indispensable in my line of work. But when I mused about these reasons, without any biases, I was convinced that smoking was a cause of stress, took up too much time because of which I couldn't give my undivided attention to work, family, or hobbies, therefore, adding more stress. I had also ignored the fact that smoking causes physical damage to the brain: any damage to the apparatus used for thinking cannot produce clearer or better thoughts. Through honest introspections, I could see that the reasons I used to justify smoking were fallacies, and therefore I no longer needed to smoke the mucky cigarettes.

Honest introspection requires that you are aware of the facts so that you can see the delusion. I have presented the findings from the latest scientific research in part one that will help with your honest introspection.

Smoke mindfully

If you are currently a smoker, mindful smoking is the single best advice you can get from this book. As I alluded to before, smoking damages your brain and dulls your mind. Here is a little experiment to prove this point. Recall the last cigarette you smoked. Try and remember the specific scenario that urged you to light up the cigarette. Some of you may attribute this to things like a telephone call or end of a stressful meeting, and others may attribute this to being part of the daily routine. Also, most of you will remember lighting up that cigarette. But can you remember the emotions you felt, the thoughts that crossed your mind, or what smoking was doing *for* you (or *to* you)? Do you remember extinguishing that cigarette? What was the thought that provoked you to smother the cigarette against the ashtray? That's right—you cannot remember. There is good science on why we have a little memory of the time between lighting up and extinguishing the cigarette that I will discuss in a later chapter on *Brain-hijacking*.

Over time smoking makes people less aware of everything around them. Smokers are consumed by the constant need to smoke—unaware that they are unable to give their full attention to the people they love. Smokers are blinded when great opportunities for growth and progress presents itself. Importantly, smokers are unable to create better opportunities because the habit has ruined their creativity and concentration. In other words, smokers cannot make the most of the opportunities that come their way— by what you might call luck—or create better opportunities through hard work.

As I write this, I remember one of my smoking buddies who was desperate for a promotion to keep up with the cost of maintaining his family. Whenever we met for a smoke and a coffee or a *smoko* as is commonly called in Australia, my friend would say: "*I really need to up my game, but I don't know what to do.*" In retrospect, smoking wasn't helping. In addition to robbing him of the little money he had, the habit was bleeding his time and creativity that could have been otherwise used to *up his game.*

Smokers are so unaware of the changes in and around them that most miss the telltale signs of the damage smoking has done to their bodies. Stand in front of the mirror and notice just how strong the yellow-brown stains on your teeth and fingers are. While you are at it, look for the signs of early aging that are caused by smoking: puffy eyes, dark circles, darkening of the skin (especially around joints of your fingers), liver spots on your skin (also called old age spots), burned lips, hair loss, wrinkles around your mouth and forehead, and gaunt hands (thin, veiny, and wrinkled hands).

Ironically, a habit that we picked up to boost our self-esteem ends up destroying precisely that. If premature aging, stained teeth, foul breath, smelly hair and clothes, lack of energy, and poor creativity does not destroy your self-esteem, there is more. If you are sexually active, consider how smoking has damaged your libido and sexual performance. Men may also notice signs of erectile dysfunction. Sure, this must hurt your self-esteem! And I did not even mention any of the painfully fatal diseases caused by smoking. I don't have to. The immediately observable effects of smoking are enough to see the full extent of the damage caused by smoking. Becoming more aware of your smoking behavior and what it is doing to you from this moment on will be a significant step towards becoming a nonsmoker.

As you read each chapter of this book, your urge to smoke may increase. My urge to smoke increased every time I typed the words *cigarettes*, *smoking*, *tobacco*, and *coffee* despite having quit for three years. But you will learn, as I have, to deal with these urges. Smoking has caused a permanent dent in the neurochemistry of our brains, and the urges will always be present. Don't fight it, and I will teach you how to deal with it less violently. So, if you feel like smoking as you read, go ahead, light it up. But you mustn't be smoking and reading at the same time. If you feel the urge, put the book down, smoke the cigarette, and then return to the book.

Starting from this moment, make smoking an exclusive habit. Don't do anything else while smoking. Don't interact with people, play with your phone, drink coffee, or eat while smoking. If you believe that smoking gives you pleasure, then you must not allow anything from disrupting the experience and derive maximum pleasure from each stick of dried tobacco leaf. Use this opportunity, and observe how you scramble when the urge to smoke hits you, how your body reacts to the smoke when you light the cigarette, feel your heart racing with each puff, and notice how your emotions change. After just a few days, you will see that smoking is anything but pleasurable.

Take baby steps

Impulsivity is what got you into the trap of smoking. Do not allow your impulsivity to derail your efforts to quit smoking by taking big, dramatic steps. To permanently quit smoking, you need to be in full control of your thoughts and action. Be more deliberate and create a plan to quit smoking taking small steps at a time. A good baby step is to self-enforce a twelve-hour smoking ban. This baby step will not help you quit smoking and will probably be stressful, but if deliberately done, it will provide the first evidence to you that quitting smoking is possible. Part two of this book is essentially a collection of baby steps. But please don't restrict your baby steps to just the ideas presented in this book. Be the best judge of your circumstances, and take the baby steps that you feel will add to the resolve to quit smoking.

The Japanese have a word for taking on a big challenge with small steps, *Kaizen* (literally translates to *change good* and its English equivalent would be *continual improvement*). *Kaizen* has an interesting history: the concept was born in Japan, but it took a whole new meaning in the United States after the great depression of 1930. Businesses, particularly in the manufacturing sector, adopted the principle of dividing the work into small tasks, most of which could be addressed on the same day. The emphasis was to improve the efficiency of each little task to enhance overall productivity. After World War II, General Douglas MacArthur's occupational forces in Japan reintroduced *Kaizen* as an inexpensive strategy to bolster Japanese businesses that were crumbling in the aftermath of the war, cash-strapped to undertake any major innovation projects.

This strategy was the foundation for the economic recovery of companies such as Toyota. *Kaizen* has gained immense popularity in recent years because of the active endorsement in the speeches of top business speakers and the publication of enormous amounts of material (business reports, books, journal articles, newspaper and magazine articles, and blogs) on the *Toyota Way* and *The Toyota Production System.* Toyota continues to use *Kaizen* to this day as a central guiding principle in its production facilities around the world. Many companies around the world have now adopted *Kaizen* as their central business philosophy.

Some of you may be questioning the relevance of *Kaizen* to breaking the habit of smoking, and that's understandable. I first read about *Kaizen* in Dr. Robert Maurer's book *The Kaizen Way* in early 2014. I didn't realize the relevance of *Kaizen* to quitting smoking until late 2015. *Kaizen* is the only simple, validated, and immediately usable process I know of where *the whole is greater than the sum of its parts.*

Most smokers rightly feel that quitting smoking is a humongous challenge. The habit takes years to develop, and smokers become dependent on smoking to deal with inconveniences and stresses of life. Smokers also depend on cigarettes to deal with their emotions. Consequently, smoking becomes an integral part of all our experiences. As you will see in later chapters, smoking is not one problem, and it has several underlying issues that need to be dealt with to prevent a relapse.

Many make the mistake of taking on the challenge of quitting with a big dramatic step. Smoking has such a powerful effect (for reasons that I will discuss later) that no single action can be big enough to prevail. Moreover, any effort to quit smoking in one big push is unlikely to help. But by far, the biggest problem is that smokers believe that it is impossible to quit smoking. Of course, I will not be able to convince you that quitting is possible and easy—no matter how hard I try. You will first have to build the confidence that you can handle the stresses of life, enjoy parties and social occasions, or that you will not be miserable after quitting smoking. I can, however, assure you that it is possible to convince anyone of these facts, and this book will help you with that.

Desmond Tutu once said that "there is only one way to eat an elephant: a bite at a time." This is how you should approach smoking cessation. Quitting smoking requires a systematic approach, and you begin by addressing one problem at a time. Each of your actions for achieving the goal of becoming a permanent nonsmoker should work synergistically to make a greater impact than what each action can individually produce. Moreover, continuously making gains over an extended period with each action will give you confidence and strengthen your resolve.

Any action you take to quit smoking must have a clear goal, be attainable in a relatively short period, and must have a defined timeline. For instance, detaching your smoking habit from the usual place of smoking is an important step in the quit smoking process. To achieve this clear goal, you might want to begin by taking your smoking breaks in different designated smoking areas throughout the day. The goal is not overly ambitious, and it can be realistically attained within a few days. You may want to set an end-of-the-week deadline to dissociate the habit from the place completely. At the end of the week, your usual place of smoking should no longer be a specific trigger for smoking. I will discuss this goal in detail in part two

We will be covering several such instances throughout the book, which will require deliberate action. If you have followed the instructions, you have already taken two baby steps towards becoming a permanent nonsmoker. Honest introspection and being mindful of your smoking behavior will pave the way for you to quit smoking permanently.

Chapter Summary

- ✓ Motivation alone is not enough to quit smoking. Determination is essential.

- ✓ Build determination by identifying obstacles and their solutions through reasoning.

- ✓ You will be able to permanently quit after you are convinced that your chances of successfully quitting are higher than failure.

- ✓ Quitting smoking needs a deliberate effort that involves three things: honest introspection, smoking mindfully, and taking baby steps.

- ✓ Honest introspection will help you see past the misinformation and stereotype of smoking.

- ✓ Being mindful about each smoking experience will help you see how cigarettes damage your self-esteem, destroy your creative thinking abilities, and is anything but pleasurable.

- ✓ Approach the process of quitting in small, deliberate steps.

- ✓ The combined effect of each small action to quit smoking must be greater than the sum of individual actions.

Part one

Understand your addiction

"Addictions...started out like magical pets, pocket monsters. They did extraordinary tricks, showed you things you hadn't seen, were fun. But came, through some gradual dire alchemy, to make decisions for you. Eventually, they were making your most crucial life-decisions. And they were...less intelligent than goldfish."

-William Gibson

What are you addicted to?

A myth is an image in terms of which we try to make sense of the world.

-Alan Watts, contemporary philosopher

hat is the difference between routine, habits, and addiction? Take brushing your teeth as an example. You clean your teeth at least once a day and around the same time. Your mouth feels dirty if you don't. Failure to immediately resolve this state will leave you with an unsettling feeling: a persistent itch that something is amiss. Smoking is much the same—you smoke every day, around the same time, and failure to do so results in a persistent itch. But why do we label one a habit and other an addiction? Since we will be using these terms repeatedly throughout the book, you must understand the difference between routine, habit, and addiction.

A routine is something you do every day. Unlike habits, routines require deliberation and effort. Paying your bills, going to work from Monday to Friday, or waking up an hour early for a morning run are examples of routines. Habits, on the other hand, are behavior that requires no conscious thought and has a degree of automaticity to them. All habits develop as a part of a routine, but not all routines develop into habits. For example, as a child, I was told to brush my teeth in the morning and before bed. Over time the routine of brushing my teeth twice a day became a habit. Similarly, washing my hands before meals or after spending time outdoors became a habit. I was also told to fold my clothes neatly and clean my room. The fact that my mother still enforces the organise-your-wardrobe-and-clean-your-room rule when I visit my parents is evidence that both folding my clothes and cleaning my room failed to become habits.

But why do some behavior become habits and others stay as routines? The answer is discomfort and distress. Any behavior that avoids discomfort and distress becomes a habit. Brushing my teeth prevented painful tooth decay, and washing my hands prevented infectious diseases. On the contrary, I was never bothered by wrinkled clothes and an untidy bedroom. Toothpaste and hand soap manufacturers have exploited our habit-forming behavior for years by advertising the prevention of tooth decay or cavities and killing "99.99 percent of germs" with their products.

Now on to the big one: addiction. It may come as a surprise to most, but addiction does not have a clear definition and is a hotly debated issue in the scientific community. According to Roy Wise, one of the top addiction experts in the world: "It [addiction] *simply means different things to different people—even to different experts.*" Therefore, you and I must agree on our working definition of addiction.

First, let's agree that addiction can occur even in the absence of a drug. Now there is gambling addiction, mobile phone addiction, internet addiction, sex addiction, and porn addiction, none of which requires ingesting or injecting a drug. Moreover, the history, phenomenology, tolerance, and neurochemical changes in the brain of a compulsive gambler or a sex addict are similar to those in drug addicts [7].

Although addiction may emerge with or without the abuse of substance, addiction in all cases must have the following five components:

1. *Positive reinforcement:* Addicted users of alcohol, marijuana, cocaine, heroin, LSD, crystal meth, and shoe polish are all drawn to the pleasure provided by their drug of choice. Pleasure is also the primary motivator of addictions such as gambling, internet, and sex addictions, none of which involve any substance abuse. The perception of pleasure positively

reinforces the behavior, and the addict keeps returning for the experience.

2. *Negative reinforcement:* For many, addiction offers an escape from the pain and misery of their current state. The perception of easing of an aversive state is a powerful motivation to engage in the addictive act repeatedly. The primary motivation for most addiction, however, is rarely to avoid distress; instead, it is to seek pleasure. But once addicted, the person may experience distressing withdrawal symptoms, including exaggeration of reality, which then serves as negative reinforcement. Addicts relieve the aversive state created by withdrawal symptoms by indulging in their addiction. Consequently, negative reinforcement is secondary in the early stages of addiction but gain greater prominence in later stages. Avoiding distress, however, is the primary driver of habits.

3. *Dependency* is a state when the addiction becomes indispensable to ensure the normal functioning of the body. Dependency can produce physical withdrawal symptoms such as cramps and pain and psychological symptoms such as depressed mood.

4. *Withdrawal symptoms* are the adverse experiences of addicts when they cannot indulge in their addiction. Common withdrawal symptoms of addiction include anxiety, restlessness, aggression, disturbed sleep, and depressed mood.

5. *Compulsive use.* I borrowed the element of compulsivity from the definition of addiction provided by the Surgeon General's report on alcohol, drugs, and health of 2016 defines addiction as: *"The most severe form of substance use disorder, associated with compulsive or uncontrolled use of one or more substances."* [8].

Both positive and negative reinforcements are subjective perceptions and vary between individuals. Dependency, withdrawal symptoms, and compulsive use are direct manifestations of subjectively perceived positive and negative reinforcement and are, therefore, also subjective perceptions. Therefore, no two addicts are alike; the level of dependency and the severity of the withdrawal symptoms depends on the addict's view of their addiction.

There is a thin line dividing addiction and habits. Both are automatic responses to a trigger and activate the reward circuits in the brain [9]. Habits can result in dependency, can have withdrawal symptoms, and can create the need for compulsive use, albeit the effect is weaker than that in addiction. Therefore, habits are relatively easier to break than addiction. But the big difference between habits and addiction is the underlying motivation to act compulsively.

Earlier I mentioned that negative reinforcement is the primary motivator for habits. Habits such as brushing teeth, washing hands, eating food, and drinking water all avoid aversive state (disease, hunger, thirst), we develop a dependency, have mild and often overlooked withdrawal symptoms (an uneasy feeling or restlessness), and we perform these actions compulsively. Other habits such as nail-biting and playing with hair may have developed as a self-consoling action to prevent extreme distress and discomfort. We may even gain some pleasure out of these habits, but that is never the underlying motivation to perform the habit. For example, you don't brush your teeth, wash your hands, take a shower each morning, or bite your nails because they give you a high, are rewarding experiences, or that make you happy. If pleasure-seeking behavior drove these habits, then you would have picked up a toothbrush—with whatever toothpaste that is currently in fashion—every time you felt blue. I am sure you will also agree that washing my hands in response to a heated argument with my wife so that I can get pleasure out of it is enough to get me a ticket to the psychiatric hospital. But some argue that they eat (or overeat) during periods of distress and this makes them happy. This is precisely why binge eating is not a habit but instead a disorder. Similarly, biting nails can be a bad habit, but when it starts being a source of pleasure, it is called onychophagia, a mental illness related to obsessive-compulsive disorder (OCD).

In contrast, addiction to alcohol, cocaine, heroin, mobile phone, pornography, and gambling are predominantly pleasure-seeking behavior. Once the addict becomes dependent, they will experience withdrawal symptoms if they cannot satisfy their addiction. The aversive state is relieved by the drug of choice or indulging in the addictive act, and the need for compulsive use arises.

In short, habits are behaviors that are repeatedly performed to avoid any pain and suffering. Addiction is a compulsive behavior that is primarily driven by a pleasurable experience. Habits also produce milder dependency, withdrawal symptoms, and the need for compulsive use than addiction.

Now to the all-important question: *is smoking a habit or an addiction?* You may have already guessed—from the detailed discussion on the difference between addiction and habit—that smoking is a habit as well as an addiction. But smoking is never both at the same time. Smoking starts as a routine, becomes an addiction, and ends up a habit.

Most smokers are motivated by the need to feel good about themselves when that start smoking. They want to feel sophisticated, cool, hip, or mature and believe that smoking is an easy way to achieve this. These are all positive reinforcements. In time, smokers begin to associate smoking with stress relief (negative reinforcement). Soon, they cannot function without cigarettes (dependency). All hell will break loose if they run out of precious cigarettes for extended periods (withdrawal symptoms). At some stage, the smoker loses control over the ability to smoke only in certain situations or at specific times in a day, and the need to compulsively smoke develops. Smoking perfectly fits the five-component definition of addiction.

But the story of cigarette addiction does not end there. As smokers gain experience, the original motivation for smoking for pleasure completely disappears. Somewhere along the way, the motivation to smoke shifts, almost exclusively, to relieving stress and retaining the ability to stay calm and focused. Seasoned smokers, without exceptions, believe that even short abstinence from smoking will make them stressed, grumpy, and distracted. Smoking then becomes more of a habit than an addiction, driven by negative reinforcement such as avoiding stress, anger, or frustration.

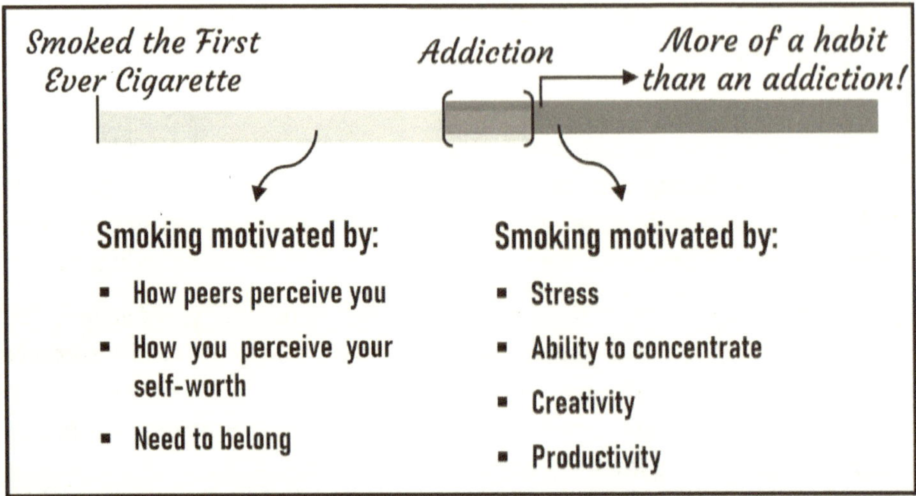

It is for this reason that we (smokers and researchers alike) are confused if smoking is a bad habit or an addiction. When smoking tick both boxes of positive and negative reinforcements, it becomes an addiction. But as our original motivations for taking up smoking such as belonging to a social circle or feeling cool and sophisticated fade with time, smokers begin to rely on cigarettes mainly to avoid or deal with stressful situations. If you have been smoking for a few years, you are no longer addicted to cigarettes. You will fail to quit if you deal with smoking as an addiction because you will be addressing the wrong problem. In the long-term, smoking is a habit, and the habit becomes stronger with time.

Then what about nicotine addiction?

Now let me address the elephant in the room—nicotine addiction. If smoking is a habit and not addiction, I should be able to prove to you beyond a reasonable doubt that nicotine addiction is a myth and that nicotine is not the underlying cause of cigarette addiction.

The concept that nicotine is the addictive component of tobacco smoke is relatively new. In 1988, the Surgeon General of the United States published its report on the health consequences of smoking and concluded that cigarettes are addictive, nicotine is to blame, and that addiction to nicotine is like being addicted to heroin or cocaine [10]. This authoritative report established nicotine, one of the seven thousand chemicals in tobacco smoke, as the cause of cigarette addiction. Since then, addiction to cigarettes has been synonymously used with nicotine addiction. The 1988 report, along with the 2010 iterations are the most cited *scientific evidence* for the addictive nature of nicotine [6]. But, researchers have criticized the Surgeon General's report for being biased [6]. The report blatantly ignored any evidence that contradicted the hypothesis that nicotine is the underlying cause of cigarette addiction. Researchers and academics are now beginning to question the nicotine addiction hypothesis [6].

It is dangerous to assume that one factor is the cause of another just because they happen to be correlated with each other. Did you know that the divorce rates in Maine perfectly correlates with the per capita consumption of margarine [11]? This does not mean that eating margarine is the cause of divorce. Similarly, just because you smoke cigarettes that contain nicotine does not mean that nicotine is necessarily the cause of the addiction. I will present three lines of scientific evidence in increasing order of strength to demonstrate that cigarettes *are* addictive, but this addictiveness *is not* due to nicotine.

The first line of evidence against the addictive nature of nicotine is ironically provided by the gold-standard, scientific, clinically-used tools to measure smoker's dependency on nicotine. The Fagerström Test for Nicotine Dependence is a standard method for measuring the intensity of physical addiction [12]. This test uses a set of six questions to measure the extent of the dependency. The six questions are:

1. How soon after you wake up, do you smoke your first cigarette?

2. Do you find it difficult to refrain from smoking in places where it is forbidden, e.g., in church, at the library, in the cinema, etc.?

3. Which cigarette would you hate most to give up?

4. How many cigarettes per day do you smoke?

5. Do you smoke more frequently during the first hours after waking than during the rest of the day?

6. Do you smoke if you are so ill that you are in bed most of the day?

The CAGE Questionnaire Modified for Smoking Behavior [13] is another method used to measure the extent of nicotine dependency. In this method, nicotine dependency is rated based on the responses to the following four questions:

1. Have you ever felt a need to cut down or control your smoking, but had difficulty doing so?

2. Do you ever get annoyed or angry with people who criticize your smoking or tell you that you ought to quit smoking?

3. Have you ever felt guilty about your smoking or about something you did while smoking?

4. Do you ever smoke within half an hour of waking up (Eye-opener)?

Psychiatrists, psychotherapists, and addiction counselors use yet another method called the 4Cs test based on the Diagnostic and Statistical Manual of Mental Disorders [14]. The 4Cs: compulsion, control, cutting down, and consequences are assessed using the following eight questions:

Compulsion

1. Do you ever smoke more that you intend?

2. Have you ever neglected a responsibility because you were smoking, or so you could smoke?

Control

3. Have you felt the need to control how much you smoke but were unable to do so easily?

4. Have you ever promised that you would quit smoking and bought a pack of cigarettes that same day?

Cutting down (and withdrawal symptoms)

5. Have you ever tried to stop smoking? How many times? For how long?

6. Have you ever had any of the following symptoms when you went for a while without a cigarette: agitation, difficulty concentrating, irritability, mood swings? If so, did the symptom go away after you smoked a cigarette?

Consequences

7. How long have you known that smoking was hurting your body?

8. If you continue to smoke, how long do you expect to live? If you were able to quit smoking today and never start again, how long do you think you might live?

Did you notice something strange about these questions that health professionals use to measure nicotine addiction? None of them even included the word nicotine, and the behavior being assessed by any of the questions can not be pinned down to nicotine. The questions set of all the three methods directly measure the dependency on cigarettes, not nicotine. Since tobacco smoke contains over seven thousand chemicals [15], it is imprudent to attribute the addictiveness of cigarettes to one chemical that makes up about a percent of the weight of a typical cigarette [16]. It is not surprising that researchers from around the world have now shown that the Fagerström Test, the gold standard to measure nicotine dependence, has poor reliability [17].

Given the chemical complexity of tobacco smoke, one may be able to argue at best that nicotine, along with other chemicals in tobacco smoke, causes addiction to cigarettes. But this argument can only be made if there is definite scientific evidence that proves nicotine causes addiction. Unfortunately, none of the clinically used tests for nicotine addiction provide that evidence. On the contrary, recent scientific studies suggest that the non-nicotine elements of smoking actively contribute to developing an addiction to cigarettes, and this leads us into the second line of evidence.

The second line of evidence that debunks the nicotine-is-the-underlying-cause-of-tobacco-addiction hypothesis comes from experiments with denicotinized cigarettes. These experiments were ignored in both 1988 and 2010 Surgeon-General's report on nicotine addiction. Denicotinized cigarettes do not contain nicotine but are otherwise visually and chemically identical to an ordinary cigarette. Studies conducted at the Duke University Medical Center at the turn of the 21st century showed that denicotinized cigarette was able to relive the cravings of long-term smokers who found these cigarettes as satisfying and rewarding as regular cigarettes [18]. Intravenous injection of pure nicotine solution reduced the craving for cigarettes but did not produce satisfaction or reward. The combination of injected nicotine and denicotinized cigarettes, however, produced similar effects as regular cigarettes [18]. Pleasure, satisfaction, and intoxication are the positive reinforcements of any drug that ultimately causes addiction. Since nicotine does not produce any of the three effects that reinforce an addictive behavior, it unquestionably cannot be the underlying cause of cigarette addiction.

The Duke University Medical Center study is not a one-off observation. There are several other studies with denicotinized cigarettes [18-26] which prove that the act of smoking itself, and not nicotine, produces pleasure, satisfaction, and reward that is generally attributed to smoking. I will discuss the details of these studies in later sections.

But it is the results of the clinical trials with nicotine replacement therapy (NRT) that provides the most persuasive argument against nicotine addiction. Yes, you read that right—the scientific studies on nicotine-containing patches, gums, and inhalers prove that nicotine is not addictive. And here is the evidence:

One of the most extensive compilations of clinical trials with NRT that included data from sixty-five thousand people showed that using any form of NRT "doubles your odds" of quitting smoking [27]. But don't get fooled by the scientific jargon. If you have a closer look at just how many people quit smoking using NRT, you will see that NRT is not as effective as you have been led to believe. Only about 7 percent of smokers using NRT remain quit at six months [28]. A quarter of these NRT users relapse after one year [29]. Finally, only 1.6 percent of smokers who use NRT remained quit in the second year [28]. Of course, the abstinence rate of 1.6 percent using NRT is better than the abstinence rate of 0.4 percent in those who did not use NRT [28]. But how can we call NRT a successful treatment for "nicotine addiction" if 98 percent of smokers remain smokers at the end of the treatment?

The authors of this study argue than the 1.6 percent abstinence rate using NRT is "expected" because the study participants had no intention to quit [28]. But if NRT was supposed to treat nicotine addiction, it should have helped smokers quit with or without any intention to quit. Intention to quit has nothing to do with addiction. Or perhaps, the poor abstinence rates can be explained by the fact that NRT's are used to treat a non-existent condition. If nicotine addiction does not exist, then it will be logical to expect the failure of NRT, and that is precisely what we see.

But research using NRT does provide another valuable piece of evidence which completely smashes the nicotine addiction myth. Pure nicotine delivered through NRT is not addictive, and the evidence is overwhelming. Several research studies show that nicotine delivered through inhalers, patch, gums, and sprays is not addictive [30-32]. Nicotine also does not cause addiction in nonsmokers [31, 33]. Nicotine delivered through NRT does not have positive or negative reinforcement, dependence or withdrawal symptoms, and any history of compulsive use.

Proponents of the nicotine addiction myth point to reports of addiction to nicotine gums in five never smokers [31], a woman in her early-40s who used nicotine gums for five years to quit smoking [34], and man in his mid-40s with a thirty-year history of high-dose nicotine gum use [35]. The advocates of the nicotine addiction myth have convinced the world of the fallacy based on a total of these seven documented cases of nicotine addiction in people using NRT from around the world in the past fifty years. Of course, they have conveniently ignored scientific research that was used to test the efficacy of NRT over the years in thousands of people, which points to the non-addictive nature of nicotine. If that is not enough, the evidence that the nicotine gums can produce non-substance addiction in some users but not a chemical addiction to nicotine has existed since

1986 [36]. More recent studies have confirmed that nicotine in gums, patches, inhalers, and nicotine-containing e-cigarettes are not addictive and do not cause any dependency [37, 38].

The scientific evidence is unequivocal. Cigarettes are addictive; nicotine is not! You may wonder why this is not common knowledge despite the availability of scientific evidence. The simple answer is that there is a significant time lag between when the scientific facts emerge and when they become part of conventional wisdom. The strongest evidence against nicotine addiction has only emerged in the past ten years.

Smokers can also look in their backyards and find the evidence against nicotine addiction. Most tobacco companies offer a low tar version of their bestselling brands of cigarettes. Tar is the oily brown substance produced as a result of burning tobacco and contains most of the seven thousand chemicals in tobacco smoke. Tar is the predominant cause of the yellow-brown stain on the fingers and teeth of smokers, emphysema, and lung cancer, among other disastrous health impacts. So far, there are no scientific reports to suggest that tar is addictive. But low tar cigarettes provide more evidence against the nicotine addiction hypothesis.

Have you ever flirted with the low tar version of your preferred cigarette brand? How did that feel? Most smokers try the low tar variants for a few days and return to their regular cigarettes. Low tar cigarettes do not give the same kick, satisfaction, or pleasure as our regular brand of cigarettes. What usually goes unnoticed is that both the regular and low tar variants contain the *same* amount of nicotine. If nicotine is the devil, we think it is, why does it not produce the same satisfaction when delivered through a low tar cigarette? That's because nicotine addiction is a myth.

Given the depth of scientific evidence and the experience of smokers, it is clear that the addictive nature of cigarettes is not due to nicotine. We cannot pin cigarette addiction on tar or any of the other six thousand nine hundred and ninety-nine chemicals in tobacco smoke. Thus, contemporary tobacco researchers attribute the addictive nature of cigarettes to the "non-nicotine components," a term so vague that it can include unicorns, Loch Ness Monster, and Santa Claus.

"But," you may say, "if nicotine does not cause addiction, how do smokers develop an addiction to cigarettes that ultimately metamorphize into a strong habit?" It's a fair question. Let's start at the beginning with the first cigarette that you ever smoked to understand how.

Chapter Summary

- ✓ Avoiding distress drives habits, and pleasure inspires addiction.

- ✓ The standard tests for nicotine addiction measure the dependency on cigarettes and not nicotine.

- ✓ People smoking denicotinized cigarette can feel the "satisfying" and "rewarding" effects of cigarettes. Pure nicotine does not produce this effect.

- ✓ Nicotine delivered through inhalers, patch, gums, and sprays is not addictive.

- ✓ People who switch to a low tar variant of the cigarette do not find it satisfying despite the two options having the same amount of nicotine.

The First Cigarette

*A cigarette is a breathing space. It makes a parenthesis.
The time of a cigarette is a parenthesis, and if it is
shared, you are both in that parenthesis. It's like a
proscenium arch for a dialogue.*

-John Berger, author of "G."

The memory of my first cigarette is as clear as the diamond on my wife's wedding ring. Ridley Scott's *Gladiator* starring Russel Crow was playing at the theaters, U2 was singing *Beautiful Day*, and Red Hot Chili Peppers had just released their hit single *Californication*. Australia's Ian Thorpe was stealing the show at the first-ever Olympics held Down Under with three golds, all of which set new world records, and two slivers. A few months later, the International Space Station received its first crew, and the second George Bush became the President-elect of the United States. And there I was, coughing so hard on a hot August afternoon that I was struggling to keep my lunch down. The vile and bitter sensation in my mouth made the matter worst. I remember the light "buzz" that lasted for twenty or thirty minutes.

The friend who offered me the first cigarette was already an experienced smoker at the time and had a good laugh at my expense. This hurt my ego a little. Determined to be a person who exudes confidence and coolness, I bought a pack of cigarettes with my pocket money on the following day and lit one up. This time I was alone. I enjoyed the feeling of holding a cigarette between my lips and taking short, shallow puffs. I felt like a superstar being able to smoke a cigarette like a man.

Most smokers remember what the first cigarette felt like. I will argue further that the experience of smoking the first cigarette may be the only one you can fully recall. Try to remember how you felt while smoking any of the subsequent cigarettes. Even better, try to remember the experience of the most recent cigarette that you smoked. How did the cigarette make you feel? What were you thinking while smoking that cigarette? How did your body react to the smoke? Don't worry if you cannot remember; the experience of the first cigarette is what matters the most. More important is the series of events that led you to light that very first cigarette.

A clear understanding of the events that created the smoker you is a crucial baby step in your journey towards becoming a nonsmoker. This understanding has at least two purposes. First, this will enable you to address your smoking behavior at its roots and completely weed it out of your life. Second, you probably still live in the same or similar environment that resulted in you lighting up the first cigarette, and relapse becomes inevitable unless you are aware of the reasons why you started smoking.

Most smokers start at a very young age. Nine out of ten smokers start smoking before they reach the age of eighteen [39-41]. But lighting up that first cigarette has several underlying reasons, some of which may have been at play from the moment you became aware of your surroundings as a child. We are continually searching for role models from an early age, both knowingly and unknowingly. We look up to someone in the family, maybe parents, older siblings, or someone close in the extended family as role models. Sometimes, they also *happen* to be smokers. In such cases, our brain considers the two facts together, and the role model for life also serves as a role model for smoking.

If you grew up in the US or Europe, and one of your parents were smokers, your chances of taking up smoking during adolescent age were almost double [42]. Smoker mothers or elder siblings tend to have a particularly strong influence on young ones to take up smoking [42]. Over seventeen thousand younglings take up smoking by the age of fifteen every year in England and Wales alone as a direct consequence of watching the immediate family smoke [42]. Researchers from Brazil, France, Ireland, Italy, the Czech Republic, and Sweden have also reported the strong impact of smokers in the immediate family on young individuals [43, 44]. At least six surveys from Italy show that over two-thirds of smokers started smoking because of the influence of family and friends [41]. The likelihood of taking up smoking increases if you shared a greater interpersonal closeness with the smoker role model [45].

Members of the social groups can have an equally resounding effect on young individuals and can serve as their role models for smoking. Reliable statistics from the Global Health Observatory Data Repository of the World Health Organization [46] show that if you were fifteen years old in the year 2000, 28 out of every 100 people you met globally was a smoker. In 2017, 21 out of every 100 people you met was a smoker. Of course, the chances of you coming across a smoker was much greater if you grew up in high tobacco burden countries such as the United States or China, where over a quarter of the population were smokers in 2000 and 2017. There are additional problems if you live in collectivistic societies such as Japan, China, Korea, Taiwan, Indonesia, Argentina, Brazil, or India, where peers have greater persuasive powers [45].

In my case, the motivation to take up smoking did not come from the family. It came from my seniors —many of whom I looked up to—in the boarding school that I attended. To me, the sight of my seniors blowing out rings of smoke in the toilets symbolized adulthood, and I couldn't wait to experience the age of ultimate freedom. When I reached high school, I marked my false realization of being a grown-up by lighting a cigarette.

Young smokers tend to heavily experiment with smoking before graduating from high school to get used to the toxic smoke [47]. Like my seniors before me, I experimented with smoking mostly in the toilets of my high school. Our gang of adolescent smokers seemed to have an endless supply of cigarettes of varying length, color, flavor, and strength. Experimenting with different kinds of cigarettes was a pleasurable experience in itself. I know that I am not alone in this experience. Toilets and dorms are smoking safe havens for teenagers all over the world [47]. This is how smoking begins as a dishonest act. Why else would one learn a pleasurable habit in stinky toilets? Young smokers also fail to see the contradiction in their thoughts and action. Most take to smoking to project an image of sophistication, cool, brave, and macho and ignore the fact that experimenting with cigarettes in toilets, dorm rooms, or dirty backstreets is gauche, cowardly, and downright disgusting.

But experimenting with smoking with friends in crummy, pest-infested locations has a stronger effect than most realize. Smoking in toilets with friends infused a sense of belonging to the tribe—scavenging the kill of the day—protected from the prying eyes of the neighboring clan. Reconnecting with the instincts of our hunter-gatherer ancestors was indeed a pleasurable experience.

This experience of belonging to the club is so overwhelming that most of us could not reject any offers to smoke even if our first smoking experience was abhorring. Studies from China, which has the largest numbers of smokers in the world, show that teens who were offered a cigarette for the very first time were more likely to accept than rejected [48]. If they disliked the first smoking experience (most do!) and reject any subsequent offer to smoke, the person making the offer was more likely to prevail [47, 48].

Smoking circles were considered elite then, and I doubt if much has changed in the past fifteen years in schools. Back in the day, young people perceived smokers as being sophisticated, wealthy, cool, and macho. Smokers had a big friend circle, and bullies usually left you alone. Even better, you were more likely to befriend the bullies as a part of the elite club. Your social status was strong as a smoker, or at least, so it seemed.

I realized the full impact of this gratifying experience of belonging to a group only when I finally quit smoking sixteen years later. I had no friends, even acquaintances, who were not smokers.

If I can go back to that fateful day, with all my experiences and knowledge accumulated since, and convince the fifteen-year-old me not to take up smoking, I will fail. There was much to gain by smoking and a lot to lose by abstaining for the fifteen-year-old me. It was not nicotine in cigarettes that sealed my status as a smoker; it was what I perceived as a sure gain of social status as a smoker and a definite loss of it as an abstainer. You will see in part two how our brain perceives losses and gains and its profound effect on smoking behavior.

Sometimes I marvel at how quickly times change. Smoking, a status symbol of the '80s and '90s that indicated affluence and sophistication, is now associated with poverty. Indeed, 80 percent of the world's billion smokers live in low- and middle-income countries [49, 50]. Even in developed countries such as the United States, people from lower-income groups spend more money on cigarettes [51]. Smokers are no longer considered as being macho or cool; instead, they are thought of as being weak-willed, irresponsible, and lacking integrity.

I remember that my parents used to have ashtrays in our living room that automatically granted visitors permission to smoke inside our house. I cannot remember when my mother removed all the ashtrays, but I think it was sometime in 1999 or 2000. In 2019, the question "do you mind if I smoke?" is almost always met with a look of annoyance and resentment from nonsmokers, all six and half billion of them. In just two decades, a strong social prop has become anti-social. I am not sure if a fifteen-year-old sees smoking as an anti-social behavior in 2019, but it surely was not perceived that way fifteen or twenty years ago.

In a way, smokers are stuck in the mindset of the past, and merely updating the mindset to the current year will be another significant baby step towards becoming a permanent nonsmoker. Just in case you have been living under a rock, in 2019, smoking is anti-social behavior. Even the tobacco industry has taken notice of this are now offering their customers cigarettes with improved smoke odor, reduced visibility of smoke, and, more recently, the smokeless and odorless "heated, not burned" cigarettes [52].

Moreover, smoking may have served as a social prop to boost your self-esteem when you started smoking as a teenager, but this is no longer the case. The visible signs of smoking on your such as stained teeth and fingers, burned lips, saggy eyes, dark circles, and skin pigmentation are aesthetically undesirable and damages your confidence and self-esteem.

This brings us to the obvious questions that we, as a society, need to ask more often. Why does a fifteen-year-old relate smoking with better social status, courage, and coolness? Why were we defenseless when the first cigarette was offered? Why could we not refuse? Parental or social peer pressure is not the only cause of young people taking up smoking. Young people don't go around lighting up a cigarette the moment they encounter a smoker for the first time. There is a significant time lag between when we first observe our smoking role models and decide to light one up ourselves. This time lag can be days, weeks, or years. What happens during this time lag is equally as crucial as social pressure in determining smoking behavior.

During this time lag, social cues that are often tactfully used as a part of a business model, reinforce a positive image of smoking. This is especially true for us millennials and centennials. The tobacco industry has bombarded us with advertisements for most parts of the 20th century: all consistently echoing the same message that smoking gives you courage and makes you look cool or sophisticated. The message came through direct advertisement or indirectly through sponsorship of popular events, especially sporting events. Can you think of a fast car and cigarettes in the same breath? Even if you are not a fan of Formula One, I am sure you can associate the red and white colors on the car with a well-known brand of cigarettes. But it was not just cars breezing through serpentine circuits in exotic locations, faster than the human body was designed to move. Cigarette advertising was rampant in baseball, cricket, football, and tennis, all of which have a massive fan following.

But, movies, perhaps more than any other medium, strengthened the positive image of smoking. Remember the badass characters played by Clint Eastwood in *For a Few Dollars More* and *The Good, the Bad, and the Ugly*? Or Bruce Willis as John McClane, the maverick New York cop in *Die Hard*? Or the indomitable character of Martin Riggs, a Los Angeles cop played by Mel Gibson in *Lethal Weapon*? Or the numerous references to smoking a cigar to mark a victorious exploit in the 1996 hit film Independence Day, which also has my favorite smoking quote from movies. Towards the end of the movie, Air Force Captain Steven Hiller (played by Will Smith) offers to smoke a cigar with David Levinson, a technological expert and environmentalist (played by Jeff Goldblum). The two light up their respective 'victory cigars,' and David asserts, "Well, it's funny. I always thought things like these would kill me," implying that there were bigger threats to human life (such as little green men with oversized heads and eyes) than smoking. The following example is the one I will invent, but every movie buff will recognize the overused movie plot of the '80s and '90s.

The baddies have cornered Jack, the protagonist, in a dimly lit room on the second floor of an abandoned warehouse. He is exhausted and outnumbered. Jack musters all his earthly courage, jumps out of the window onto the ground floor shattering the glass in the process. Blood drips down his face as the bad guys run towards him. He single-handedly takes them on. The fistfight continues for a considerable length of time until only two baddies remain. Seeing that their army was no match for Jack, the two villains now bear an intense expression of fear on their faces. They reach for their guns and start to fanatically shower their surprisingly never-ending stock of bullets in the general direction of Jack. Jack runs for cover behind a pillar. The villains continue to shoot, hoping one of the rounds will magically penetrate the concrete pillar. Luckily for Jack, the fallen baddies had dropped their guns conveniently close. Jack reaches for the guns while successfully dodging the stream of bullets. He checks if the weapon is loaded and finds that the first one is out of bullets. The second gun, fortunately, had two unfired rounds.

Dramatic music fades in. Jack has a hopeless look on his face. He reached for the pack of cigarettes in his left pant pocket. The two villains stop shooting. Dramatic music continues. Jack emerges in slow motion from behind the battered pillar, now with a bold and confident look on his face, a cigarette in his mouth, and a gun in each of his hands. He only has one shot at this. The fifteen-year-old you are at the edge of your seat gripped in the action sequence. Jack squeezes the triggers. Dramatic music fades into silence. A second later, the two baddies drop to the ground with a thud. Suddenly, Jack falls in exhaustion. The police arrive just in time (along with fire trucks and ambulances). Jack, fully recovered after receiving first-aid, walk into the sunset, smoking his cigarette.

The movie ends. But even without you realizing it, the life of a smoker has just begun for you. Do not underestimate the impact of movies on the soon-to-be-smoker. Frequent exposure to smoking scenes in movies doubles the odds of young people taking up smoking [53].

We are exposed to these not-so-subtle visual cues from a very young age that reinforces the idea that smoking somehow makes us brave, unleashing our physical and mental capacity, and help us cope with our problems better. In the next five to ten years, when you start experiencing the stresses of life, and you do not like your chances, you reach for a stress buster. The same stress buster that enabled John, Martin, Captain Hiller, and Jack to overcome their powerful adversaries and the only one you have ever known: A cigarette!

Popular music groups of the '80s and '90s also promulgated the cool and collected image of a smoker. If you are a fan of rock music, you will remember Slash, the lead guitarist of *Guns N' Roses*, playing the guitar solo in front of a church in the music video of the hit song *November Rain* flaunting his trademark black top hat and cigarette between his lips. Frontmen of almost all legendary rock bands: Axl Rose (*Guns N' Roses*), Freddy Mercury (*Queen*), Jimmy Hendrix, David Lee Roth (*Van Halen*), Matt Bellamy (*Muse*), and Vince Neil (*Mötley Crüe*) to name a few have appeared in popular videos smoking their cigarettes [fn04]. If you were not into rock, you would undoubtedly remember George Michael or Madonna. More recent artists seen clutching to their cigarettes include Chris Brown, Zayan Malik (*One Direction*), Lady Gaga, Britney Spears, Miley Cyrus, Katy Perry, Rihanna, Adele, and Cheryl Cole but this list is virtually endless. These artists command a huge fan following and have a significant impact on the current trends in our society.

But isn't it amazing how the tobacco industry gets people—family, friends, and celebrities—to pay through their nose for a product that at

---

[fn04] These are some of my favorite bands. I still listen to their music every day, but they no longer cast a positive image of smoking for me. Slash, the lead guitarist of Guns N' Roses, was also an inspiration for me to learn guitar and I had posters of him all over my room. One of my friends once asked what I would do if I ever met Slash to which I responded by saying "I will put a cigarette in his mouth." I truly believed then than the guitar playing genius was a product of smoking and didn't see the hard work behind his skill.

best leads to severe health problems when used as intended and then advertise the product to the younger generation for free? The information is communicated in such a way that to a fifteen-year-old, smoking means adulthood, freedom, brave, cool, and macho. This temptation is what gets us to light up the very first cigarette and cement our status as a smoker.

So far, we have taken the *let's blame it on others* approach to explaining our smoking behavior. To ensure fair play, we must introspect deeper and see ourselves in the mirror. Sure, some of us were affected by peer-pressure, influenced by social cues and advertisements, or both. But no one forced us to hold the cigarette between our fingers, take it between your lips, roll the lighter with the other hand, and take a puff committing to a lifetime of slavery. Certainly, no one forced me to smoke, and this is true for most, if not all, smokers.

Many smokers picked up their first cigarette as a sign of rebellion. Smoking was a way of sticking it to the Man, be it parents, teachers, or even the law. Smoking is forbidden by law under a certain age (under eighteen years in most and twenty in some countries) or by parents irrespective of your age. The combination of restricted access and the cool image projected by smoking role models makes this dirty habit even more irresistible. I know because this is exactly what happened to me, and possibly to most smokers. The fifteen-year-old me had the toxic combination of rebellious attitude and poor self-esteem, and I desperately wanted to conform to the prevailing social norms when I first took up smoking.

I understand it is difficult for most of us to accept the fact that we suffered from varying degrees of poor self-esteem before lighting up the cigarette. The image of a smoker being tough and cool was at play for most smokers, particularly among those who started young, and we saw cigarettes as a solution to our problem. Other issues that hurt your self-esteem, such as physical appearance, mediocre academic performance, bullying, and discrimination, may have also played a significant role in establishing your smoking behavior [54, 55].

Realizing and accepting the root cause of my smoking problem was incredibly liberating because I could then compare the personality of the fifteen-year-old and the twenty-five-year-old me.

The fifteen-year-old me lacked self-esteem, needed to conform to social norms, and was easy to influence. I had poorly developed mental faculties for long-term planning, decision-making, problem-solving, and self-control as the part of the brain that regulates these functions only mature around the mid-20s. (I will be discussing the maturity of brain functions in the next chapter).

By the time I turned twenty-five, my self-esteem was soaring, I no longer felt the need to conform, had developed an independent identity, could control external influences better, and my mental faculties of planning and self-control had fully matured. Heck, there was nobody left to rebel against. Authority figures such as parents and teachers accepted me as an adult and did not interfere much in my life. I was of legal age to smoke cigarettes. So, rebel against whom? As a university professor and a parent, I have swapped chairs with the fifteen-year-old me. Students rebel against my classroom rules every day, and in just a few short years, I will be witnessing a rebellious daughter at home. What goes around does come around!

So, if the circumstances that made smoking an attractive choice for the fifteen-year-old me no longer existed after my mid-20s, why did I continue to smoke into my 30s? The gain of social status and feeling mature, cool, and sophisticated immediately after smoking that first cigarette ticked the first box of positive reinforcement: a step closer towards addiction. Cigarettes soon become the one-stop solution for dealing with anything: emotions, problems, inconveniences, time management, and even laziness. This is where the negative reinforcements that were largely irrelevant in the early days of a smoker come into the picture. You smoke to avoid an emotional meltdown, overshooting a deadline, and boredom [fn05]. Most importantly, smoking becomes a way to

---

[fn05] Compared to those smoking for stress relief or improving productivity, a smaller percentage of men and women smoke cigarettes to relief boredom [56, 57]. But I have never really

deal with stressful situations. Smoking then ticks the second box of negative reinforcement and becomes an addiction. Soon, the pleasure of smoking will fade, and you will be smoking mostly for relaxing. In the next chapter, I will discuss how smoking transitions from addiction to a habit and its all-important relationship with stress.

Chapter Summary

✓ Influences from family and friends played a significant role in you taking up smoking.

✓ Tobacco advertising successfully created a positive image of smoking.

✓ Smoking symbolized courage, sophistication, wealth, coolness, and machismo.

✓ Smokers take to smoking to bolster their self-esteem.

✓ Ironically, visible signs of smoking, such as signs of early aging and skin pigmentation, end up destroying one's self-esteem.

✓ In the current day and time, smoking has become an anti-social behavior.

✓ Smoking is associated with poverty, lack of civility, and being weak-willed in the 21st century.

✓ When we start using smoking to deal with our day-to-day problems, it becomes more of a habit than an addiction.

understood this. What makes smoking so interesting that it can relief boredom?

Task #1
Why did you start smoking?

✓ It is very important to put your thought into words, so I urge you to make a list of the reasons why you started smoking all those years ago.

✓ It's ok if you do not remember all the reasons. As and when you think of more reasons, come back to this page and update the list.

✓ If you are reading the digital version of this book, please create this list in your favorite notes-keeping app.

Is this reason still relevant today?

1. _______ YES _ NO _____

2. _______ YES _ NO _____

3. _______ YES _ NO _____

4. _______ YES _ NO _____

5. _______ YES _ NO _____

6. _______ YES _ NO _____

7. _______ YES _ NO _____

8. _______ YES _ NO _____

9. _______ YES _ NO _____

10. _______ YES _ NO _____

Brain-hijacking

Smoking is the leading cause of statistics.

-Fletcher Knebel, bestselling author of "Seven Days in May"

A large chunk of the brain's firepower is dedicated to avoiding unsafe environments the moment we embarked on that epic swim across the birth canal. The brain continually scans for threats, and if it finds one, it will perform the triple task of information processing, storage, and response. Though, the brain deals with low-to-moderate level and high-level threats differently.

A typical response to a low-to-moderate intensity threat is very calculated, deliberate, and non-repeatable. For example, if you run out of sugar for your morning coffee, your immediate reaction will be that of surprise or frustration (oh my god!). You may then choose to drink coffee without sugar this one time or skip your coffee and remember to buy sugar later that day. These thought processes, triggered by the discovery that you have run out of sugar, provided temporary relief (I will skip coffee) and set a reminder to resolve the problem by buying sugar later that day so that you avoid such silly issues in life. Any response to low-to-moderate intensity threat, no matter how frequently you encounter them, is not stored by the brain and, therefore, does not become habits. Consequently, you run out of sugar every once in a while.

But if the brain perceives a high-level threat, that is, your survivability is at stake, the brain tries to avoid it altogether. Under high-level threat, your brain takes full control of the body and redirects all of its resources to protect you from harm. If you are encountering a particular threat for the first time, the brain will store and automate your response so that you can respond quickly to avert a similar threat in the future. Due to the limited real estate in the brain, it prioritizes storing our responses to high-level threats that end up becoming habits—behaviors that are instinctively performed to avoid distress and discomfort. For example, what do you do if you are crossing the street with your head buried in your smartphone and hear a loud honk? You jump out of the way when you see a huge truck speeding toward you. You don't think or plan this response; you react instinctively to avert the threat.

Although we are born with this threat response system at birth, we learn to perceive a threat and its appropriate response by experience or observation. At some point, you learned that the collision with a speeding truck could be fatal, and the appropriate response is to get our of the way quickly. My daughter, who only recently learned to walk, does not recognize a speeding car as a threat yet and is always trying to run on the streets. She does not have to get hit by a car to learn that this is dangerous. She will learn by observing our words and actions over time that it is dangerous to run on the road full of speeding cars. She learned to avoid other threats such as a hot object by experience. But once she learns to perceive a high-level threat and how to avoid it, the response becomes automatic.

Smoking ultimately ends up hijacking this threat response system. The first cigarette solved a problem. Irrespective of the nature of the problem, I am certain that the problem solved by smoking for most smokers was not of low-to-moderate intensity. Even social pressure and low self-esteem that some may regard as a low-to-moderate intensity problem pose a high threat to our survivability. We are social animals, and our self-esteem plays a crucial role in determining our position in society. For most of us, smoking was a tool to address social pressure by rebelling or projecting the image of sophistication, maturity, toughness, and coolness. Relieving the social pressure by smoking gave a boost to our self-esteem and made us more acceptable in social circles. As a result, smoking immediately expanded our social circle, which boosted our self-esteem even more, and we felt good about our actions.

All smokers learn to tag smoking as a viable solution to our problems through trial and error. The chances are that you tried addressing any self-esteem issue by other means such as funky hairstyles or dressing in the latest fashion before settling on cigarettes. But you also learn to use cigarettes to avoid or resolve potential threats by observing people around you, just the way my eighteen-months-old daughter is learning to perceive and avoid threats by observation. You have seen parents, siblings, friends, actors, musicians, artists, inventors, and writers deal with their problems in life with cigarettes. When you lit the first cigarette, you validated what you have learned through observation and experience—smoking helps us solve problems or at least help deal with them better.

Towards the end of the previous chapter, I asked the question: if the original reasons for taking up smoking no longer exists, why do we continue to smoke? The simple answer is that we learn to associate smoking as a solution or a part of the solution to what we perceive as threats, and the brain automates this threat response system. *It is the automaticity that establishes smoking a strong habit.*

Once smoking becomes a part of the automatic threat response system, the brain attempts to match smoking as a potential solution to other problems of similar nature [fn06]. The brain analyzes past experiences, thought patterns, emotions, and actions associated with poor self-esteem and spits out a feeling you have repeatedly had during your bouts of poor self-esteem or intense social pressure. It analyzes further. It is a feeling that you have experienced since birth with no predictable solution so far. The brain has just matched smoking as a lucrative solution to stress. This is when the process of addiction starts. Once addicted, smoking hijacks your threat response system, and the brain begins to senselessly assign a high-threat label to anything that deviates from the usual state: deadlines,

---

[fn06] The brain is always trying to reduce its workload by trying to match existing and newly discovered solutions to unsolved problems.

arguments, late for work, unexpected events, or any other situation that has the potential to even slightly increases your stress level. Over time, smoking becomes an integral part of your threat response system, and you feel weak and vulnerable without it.

It is not surprising that the number one reason smokers give to justify smoking is that it de-stresses them. Numerous research studies show that stress is one of the biggest reasons why people across the world smoke [43, 56-65]. Even in the absence of scientific evidence, all smokers will swear that smoking helps them deal with stressful situations better and that it relaxes them. I certainly would have for most parts of the sixteen years as a smoker.

Before we dwell on how smoking relieves stress, you need to understand how stress works under the hood. Stress is an intrinsic part of our threat response system; it is the brain's way of telling the rest of the body that a threat has been perceived and simultaneously prepares the body to avoid the threat. In other words, stress makes the body combat-ready. When we encounter a stressful event such as an impending head-on car collision, a poisonous redback spider, failing in a test, or unable to meet a work-related deadline, the brain perceives this as a threat to our existence and initiates a neuronal signal from the part of the brain known as the amygdala. The amygdala is an almond-shape clump of neurons located deep in the brain and is the emotion procession center of the brain.

After detecting a potential threat, the amygdala sends a distress call to the command center of the brain—the hypothalamus—that can quickly send messages to the rest of the body. Neither amygdala nor the hypothalamus investigates the potential threat to verify if it does pose a real danger. As soon as the hypothalamus receives the distress signal, it increases your breathing rate and, therefore, oxygen supply. The hypothalamus sends another signal to release sugars and fats into the bloodstream from storage sites in the body for extra energy. Another signal increases blood flow to vital organs by increasing heart rate and blood pressure. You are now in survival mode, ready to fight for your life or fly away from danger. These changes happen so quickly that the brain has not yet thoroughly evaluated the situation. As a result, most people jump out at the very sight of a harmless cockroach!

As the body prepares to deal with the threat, the hypothalamus also alters brain function, particularly of the prefrontal cortex, which sits square above your eyes. The prefrontal cortex is the most highly evolved part of the human brain and performs what is known as the *executive function* that includes encoding and retrieval of memory, planning, decision-making, problem-solving, self-control, and acting with long-term goals in mind [66]. The prefrontal cortex also suppresses short-sighted and impulsive behavior to make way for the executive functions. The prefrontal cortex is extremely sensitive to stress, and even minor inconveniences can dramatically alter its functions [67]. Under stressful conditions, the hypothalamus shuts down the prefrontal cortex so that we can make quick, impulsive decisions and actions [68]. In short, stress shuts down critical thinking and reasoning and activates automatic, spontaneous responses. Although the decisions and actions may be error-prone [68], being quick and impulsive is crucial for survival in dire situations [fn07].

The areas of the brain that processes emotions such as the amygdala and the hypothalamus fully develop during adolescence, but the prefrontal cortex continues to grow and only matures as one approaches the age of twenty-five [69]. Thus, our emotional drive is fully matured during adolescence, whereas the capacity for suppressing impulsive behavior, planning, decision-making, and self-control are still developing. It is because of this poorly developed mental faculty of self-control that most smokers impulsively light their first cigarette in their adolescent years. Consequently, smoking is an incredibly emotional experience that defies logic and reason.

Smoking has two very specific effects on the brain. First, when you extinguish a cigarette, it creates a depressed mood [70]. Second, the prefrontal cortex becomes dependent on smoking to work in its normal efficiency [69, 71, 72]. Research in the past five years has shown that

---

[fn07] This is at least how the brain perceives it. During the course of our evolution, the brain has had to deal with predators and accidents that is unheard of in this day and time. For most parts of our existence, we have fended such threats with quick impulsive actions. Years of evolution has engraved this flight or fight response in our brain.

withdrawal from smoking for as little as a few hours suppresses the prefrontal cortex and, therefore, its executive functions [73-77]. Consequently, your prefrontal cortex activity drops as the effect of the last cigarette fades; your ability for self-control is gone, impulsivity takes over, you become less efficient in making decisions or solving problems, and the future becomes inconsequential. Fortunately, this dependency of the prefrontal cortex on smoking to perform its executive functions can be fully reversed within six months of quitting [78].

As a scientist, I find the effect of smoking on the prefrontal cortex as elegant as the intricate design of the human eye. Smoking hijacks the brain in such a way that when the impact of the last cigarette fades, your mood becomes depressed, the ability to resist is temporarily unavailable, you are unable to think your way out of it, or care if smoking will cause cancer in the future. You light a cigarette, your mood is normalized, and the three things that can keep you away from smoking—reasoning, self-control, and future consequence—becomes functional again. Ever wondered why the motivation to quit is the highest towards the end of the cigarette we are currently smoking or immediately after we have smoked? Well, now you know why. But as the effects of the last cigarette fade, the executive function of the prefrontal cortex wanes again—killing all motivations to quit—and you reach for another cigarette.

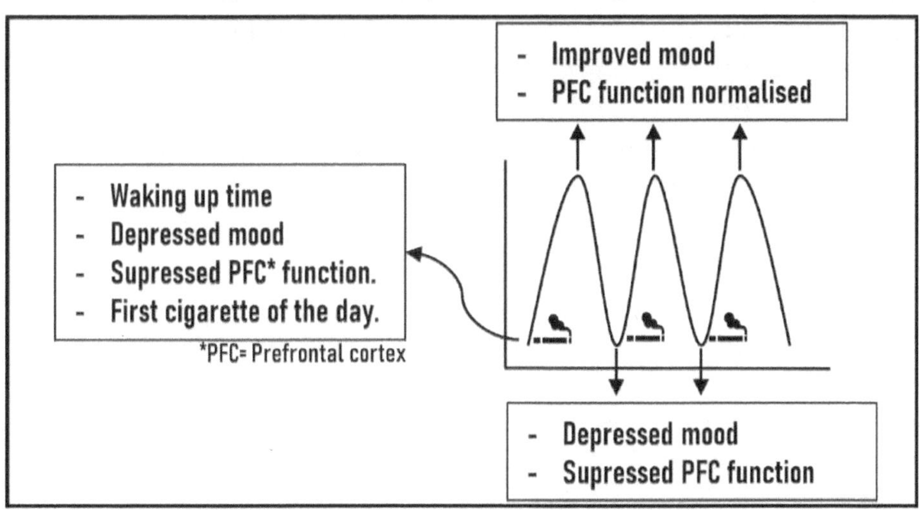

Earlier I said that stress shuts down the prefrontal cortex. The prefrontal cortex is also suppressed between cigarettes, tricking your brain into believing that it is experiencing a stressful situation. This illusion of stress confuses the brain.

Under genuine stress conditions (such as when confronted by a hungry lion), the prefrontal cortex is naturally suppressed and enables us to make quick, impulsive actions (*don't think, RUN!* response). When the threat is removed (the lion is out of sight), the stress response is no longer necessary, and the functioning of the prefrontal cortex (rational thinking and self-control) returns to normal.

Now compare the genuine stress response with the brain's stress response to smoking. As the effect of the last cigarette fades, the activity of the prefrontal cortex declines to below optimal levels, which inhibits reasoning and self-control and causes impulsivity. This change in brain activity causes the illusion of stress, except there is no real threat (lion) to run away from or remove from the surroundings. The smoker lights up a cigarette instinctively to relieve the depressed mood (*don't think, SMOKE!* response) and restores the normal functioning of the prefrontal cortex, and the illusion of stress goes away. And what happens when the effect of this cigarette fades? That's right; you smoke another cigarette. Smoking only relieves the depressed mood and the illusion of stress that it creates in the first place! You go in circles of experiencing depressed mood that is relieved by the next cigarette, followed by another bout of depressed mood that demands another cigarette. The only way to escape this cycle is by breaking the chain and implementing a *don't smoke, THINK!* response instead of the usual *don't think, SMOKE!* response. The next time you feel like lighting up a cigarette, please stop for a moment and consider that perhaps the cigarette is the hungry lion you ought to run away from.

"But," you may ask, "if smoking tricks the brain into a stress response, and stress is the brain's way of telling the body that it has detected a threat, shouldn't the body show signs of stress after smoking?" It sure does. Several studies show that smoking reduces psychological stress and anxiety based on smoker's subjective perception of stress [79-83]. These studies also show that smoking increases heart rate and blood pressure after smoking and at rest, which are signs of physiological stress [81, 82, 84]. The body manifests physical symptoms of stress because smoking tricks the brain into believing that it is experiencing a stressful event. Cigarettes seem to both relieve and create stress. This dual effect of smoking on stress is known as *Nesbitt's paradox* after Paul Nesbitt, who first described the phenomenon in 1973 [79].

After evaluating a large volume of relevant research data, British psychologist Andrew Parrott concluded that *"..the positive changes noted by Nesbitt and Schachter (relaxation and alertness), largely reflect the reversal of the negative effects of abstinence (irritability and impaired concentration)."* [85]. In other words, smoking only relieves the stress created by the last cigarette. Data from hundreds of studies have demonstrated that cigarettes do not make you less stressed or more alert than a nonsmoker; it merely relieves the depressed mood and stress caused by the ending of the last cigarette [70, 85]. Consequently, a billion smokers feel that smoking relieves their stress but fail to see that cigarette is what caused the stress in the first place.

Smoke mindfully, one of my three original instructions, was based on these changes in the brain with smoking. Your ability to think, decide, or solve problems peaks immediately after a cigarette, and the future consequences of your actions become relevant again. This puts you in the best mental shape to plan a quit-smoking strategy (discussed in part two).

There is another reason to smoke mindfully; the brain-hijacking by cigarettes is so thorough that it corrupts the smoker's view of the world. The highs of life do not feel as good, and the lows seem lower than they are for a smoker because of the depressed mood caused by the ending of the last cigarette. This gives birth to exaggerations and myths. Isn't it amazing what smokers consider to be a stressful situation? A telephone call, going to the bank, posting a letter, responding to an email, taking their children to the park, going to work, train delayed by few minutes, paycheck delayed by few hours, or attending a wedding. Aren't these blatant exaggerations? I know that many smokers will contest that these are indeed stressful experiences (I used to be one of those smokers). Perhaps the hypochondriac behavior of smokers is a more convincing example of smokers exaggerating the severity of their situations. Remember how the skin rash was most likely skin cancer; the sore throat, persistent cough, and pain while swallowing food was emphysema; the lump you discovered was certainly a tumor (or worst), and the piercing pain in the chest after a particularly heavy lunch was a mild heart attack. If you are still not convinced that smokers exaggerate the minor things in life, including their smoking behavior, I am sure that you will be by the time you finish reading the next chapter.

Chapter Summary

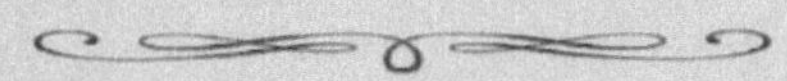

✓ The brain considers smoking as a solution to threats and stores it as an automatic response.

✓ The next time you experience a situation that the brain perceives as a serious threat, you habitually reach for a cigarette.

✓ The prefrontal cortex controls planning, decision-making, problem-solving, self-control, and foresight.

✓ Most smokers impulsively take to smoking during adolescence as the prefrontal cortex only matures in the mid-20s.

✓ Since the emotion-processing center of the brain mature much earlier, smoking becomes an impulsive but incredibly emotional experience.

✓ The prefrontal cortex becomes dependent on smoking and is suppressed between cigarettes to create the illusion of stress without a stressor.

✓ Smoking only relieves the illusion of stress caused by cigarettes in the first place. Smokers are not less stressed than non-smokers.

Task #2
Why do you currently smoking?

✓ Before you go on to read the next chapter, spend some time to compile a list of reasons why you currently smoke. To make sure that your list is as exhaustive as possible, ask the same question in different ways.

- Why do I want to smoke?

- What does smoking do for me?

- What do I like about smoking?

- What would life be like without cigarettes?

1. ____

2. ____

3. ____

4. ____

5. ____

6. ____

7. ____

8. ____

9. ____

10. ____

Stupefied!

A cigarette is the perfect type of a perfect pleasure. It is exquisite, and it leaves one unsatisfied. What more can one want?

-Oscar Wilde, poet and playwright

n earlier chapters, we looked at why smokers picked up the very first cigarette, developed a dependency, and the role stress plays in this process. But I am sure that you listed many more items in addition to stress as the reasons why you currently smoke in the task I left you with at the end of the previous chapter. Did you include things such as smoking makes me more creative or productive, it improves my concentration, or I have an addictive personality? In this chapter, I want to challenge the reasons why people smoke despite losing all their original reasons for smoking and a fully developed brain that has the same capacity as any other to suppress impulsivity and exercise self-control.

You must read this chapter autobiographically. I invite you to introspect as I challenge the common reasons smokers give to justify their smoking habit. Expand the arguments with your insights. Ignore the arguments that are not relevant to you. But make this chapter all about you.

To help you make the most of this chapter, it is best if I give you some clear objectives. The sole purpose of this chapter is to analyze if your current reasons to smoke are genuine or are simply an exaggeration of actualities. Of course, I will argue that all the reasons smokers give to justify smoking are exaggerations, but I want the evidence presented in the subsequent sections to convince you. When smoking makes no logical sense, and there is nothing left to sustain or justify your smoking behavior, I truly believe that you will quit smoking. As much as we are emotional as a species, we are also logical and rational beings. Therefore, I expect that many of you will quit at the end of this chapter. If you feel that you have no chance of relapsing and have a plan to deal with any potential issues post-quitting, then you don't have to read part two of this book (As I said before, I have no interest in wasting an iota of your time.).

I also know that smoking can make strong people shake in their pants, and I have firsthand experience of the physical and psychological bond between smokers and their cigarettes. If you have any doubt whatsoever in your commitment and capacity to quit, please continue to read part two.

If you are a current smoker, do not read beyond this paragraph unless you have just smoked a cigarette. If not, please step out, smoke your cigarette, and then return to read the following sections of this chapter. Also, postpone reading the rest of this chapter if you don't have the opportunity to smoke for another hour or so. I estimate that the average reader will be able to read and think about the pieces of evidence and arguments to follow in about ninety minutes. I need your prefrontal cortex to be running in full capacity so that you can rationally digest the information I am about to give. My original instructions still apply: do not read and smoke at the same time. Put down the book, smoke your cigarette, and then continue reading after.

Reason to smoke #1: "Cigarette relieves my stress."

Although I have dealt with stress and smoking in the previous chapter, it merits further discussion outside the neurological and physiological contexts. If you recall from the previous chapter, there is scientific evidence that smoking relieves stress and anxiety based on the subjective rating of the smoker, but physiological measurement suggests that smoking causes stress. It is, therefore, crucial to understand how and why smokers subjectively perceive stress and the impact of smoking on this perceived stress.

After my last failed quit attempt, I deeply introspected on why I had failed. I had quit for about three months without feeling the slightest urge to light up a cigarette. But when a situation that I had previously labeled stressful presented itself, I relapsed. For instance, I suddenly felt stressed before the first lecture of the semester and experienced a particularly strong urge to smoke. Since my earliest memory, I wanted to be a teacher. I believe that this is my calling, and I enjoy my work. Then why was I stressed before the first lecture of the semester, I wondered.

Another situation where I resorted to smoking after weeks of abstinence is when one of my old smoking buddies reached out to me for help. He was experiencing clinical depression at the time. My thought when I met him was that if I don't smoke with him as we used to in the past, he will feel guilty that he hasn't quit, and this will further aggravate his depression. I know what most of you are thinking but what better evidence than this to show that stupidity and a bloated sense of self-worth come freely with smoking.

Somehow this line of introspection mushroomed, and I began questioning everything I believed about smoking. How can a casual or intellectual talk with a friend be stressful? Why does a telephone call trigger the craving for a cigarette? Or why smoking is an automatic response to a disagreement with a colleague or my wife? Certainly, these situations do not pose a severe threat to our survival. Then why is it that our instinctive response in such situations is to light a cigarette? Are these events real stressors, or did I invent them to justify smoking?

During these introspections, I revisited Leo Tolstoy's essay "*Why Do Men Stupefy Themselves?*" which I hadn't read since high school. In it, Tolstoy, also a smoker, beautifully sums up the effect of tobacco as follows:

> *What distinguishes tobacco from most other stupefiers, besides the ease with*
> *which one can stupefy oneself with it and its apparent harmlessness, is its*

portability and the possibility of applying it to meet small, isolated occurrences that disturb one.

Excerpt from "Why Do Men Stupefy Themselves?" by Leo Tolstoy

The more I think about it, the more I become convinced that as smokers, we become very good at inventing stressful events to justify smoking. Think about all the stressful events that trigger the urge to smoke: an argument with your partner, an impending deadline, a disagreement with a co-worker, a nagging child, a telephone call, an email, or meeting a potential client. These are not real stressors; they are *expected* disruptions to our usual state. Smokers feel an urge to smoke anytime they deviate from their usual state and subsequently label these events stressful.

As discussed in the earlier chapter, once your brain registers an event as being stressful, your automatic threat response system will trigger the urge to smoke when you experience a similar situation in the future. Authors Charles Duhigg (*The Power of Habit, Random House UK*) and James Clear (*Atomic Habit, Random House Business Books*) call this the habit loop. The habit loop has four distinct components: cue, craving, response, and reward. A habitual response automatically sets off when we encounter a familiar *cue* or *trigger*. This will induce a *craving* that can only be relieved by executing the learned *response*. Finally, the brain releases neurochemicals to make the execution of the habit loop a *rewarding experience*.

During the formation of a habit, initial repetition, or exposure to a context creates an imprint in the memory of the typical response [86]. For example, in the early years of your smoking habit, if you took to smoking every time you disagreed with somebody, your brain registered smoking as a typical response to disagreements. Once the habit is firmly established, it becomes an automatic response. Every time you experience the context in the future, you will act without even thinking about it like a trained laboratory rat.

Remember how I said that a big chunk of your brain's firepower is dedicated to scanning for threats and avoiding them? To save the brain the time and efforts from reinventing the wheel, an equally large dollop is dedicated to creating automatic responses to repetitive tasks. The brain incentivizes performing the habit by activating the reward pathways, thereby strengthening its automaticity.

But here is a zinger with habits. The automatic response to a familiar context does not necessarily modify the context itself. All it does is complete a set of automatic actions. For example, disagreement with a co-worker (context) would fire the automatic response of stress that needs to be resolved by smoking. Following this template, as instructed by the brain, gives you a brief neurochemical high as a reward. The context, in this case, the disagreement with a co-worker, is unchanged by the response.

Although the brain activates the response of stress automatically, the act of smoking is not at all automatic. You need to move out of your current physical location, find a place to smoke, and if you don't have cigarettes on you, find a place to buy them. Moreover, you have just lost time in the unproductive act of smoking. Aren't each of these steps stressful in themselves?

Nevertheless, you get back to work after smoking the cigarette and try and diffuse the situation with your co-worker. But you are now worried that the dirty smell of cigarettes will bother your co-worker, and you try to mask the smell with mints. (Just in case you are not aware of this mints do not cancel the smell of burned tobacco; you smell of mint and cigarettes.) Later, you are worried if your co-worker is judgmental about your smoking habit. You rush out and light up another cigarette to douse your insecurities. Sounds familiar?

Smokers invent stressful reasons to smoke, stressfully participate in the act of smoking, add more stress by trying to mask the smell, and smoke another one to deal with the additional stress while the original stressor remains untouched. Smoking does not decrease stress; smoking causes stress. Smoking-induced stress works like compound interest—each time you activate a smoking response, it compounds your stress perpetually. Think about it: don't you have more stress, more work, and less time than your non-smoking partner or friends?

Many smokers attempt to break their bad habit by altering the cue, response, or reward of the habit loop. But once an action has been repeated several times to a cue and becomes a habit, you cannot modify it. For example, if you smoke in response to an argument with your partner, you cannot substitute smoking by listening to music. All you can do is suppress the argument-smoking habit consciously and create new habit such as argument-music. But the old habit will remain in the archives of your brain, priming you for relapse in the future unless you create a way to deal with it. I will show you how in the second part of this book.

To sum up,

- Most of the events we label as being stressful are just a ruse to smoke a cigarette.

- Irrespective of the genuineness of the stressor, smoking does not modify the original problem.

- The act of smoking itself is very stressful.

- Replacing an element of the habit loop does not alter the habit. It creates another habit.

Reason to smoke #2: "Cigarette helps me focus, makes me creative, and productive."

I may know a thing or two about creativity (a requirement in my line of work), but I must admit that I am no expert on the subject. But Leo Tolstoy, one of the greatest writers of all time, was undoubtedly a creative genius. While the quote from his essay *"Why Do Men Stupefy Themselves?"* that I referred to a few pages ago is still fresh in your memory, here is another one from the same essay.

It is usually said (and I used to say) that smoking facilitates mental work.
And that is undoubtedly true if one considers only the quantity of one's
mental output. To a man who smokes, and who consequently ceases strictly
to appraise and weigh his thoughts, it seems as if he suddenly had many

thoughts. But this is not because he really has many thoughts, but only because he has lost control of his thoughts.

When a man works he is always conscious of two beings in himself: the one works, the other appraises the work. The stricter the appraisement the slower and the better is the work; and vice versa, when the appraiser is under the influence of something that stupefies him, more work gets done, but its quality is poorer.

"If I do not smoke I cannot write. I cannot get on; I begin and cannot continue," is what is usually said, and what I used to say. What does it really mean? It means either that you have nothing to write, or that what you wish to write has not yet matured in your consciousness but is only beginning dimly to present itself to you, and the appraising critic within, when not stupefied with tobacco, tells you so. If you did not smoke, you would either abandon what you have begun, or you would wait until your thought has cleared itself in your mind; you would try to penetrate into what presents itself dimly to you, would consider the objections that offer themselves, and would turn all your attention to the elucidation of the thought.

But you smoke, the critic within you is stupefied, and the hindrance to your work is removed. What seemed insignificant to you when not inebriated by tobacco, again seems important; what seemed obscure no longer seems so; the objections that presented themselves vanish and you continue to write, and write much and rapidly.

Excerpt from "Why Do Men Stupefy Themselves?" by Leo Tolstoy

I couldn't agree with Tolstoy more. One of the obvious effects of quitting smoking was the dramatic improvement in my capacity to think clearly, and I was able to focus for extended periods. I don't believe that it was something in the tobacco smoke that stifled my mental abilities. Instead, it was the frequent breaks I had to take for smoking while at work. These breaks were having a much greater impact on the quality of my work than what I could imagine three years ago as a smoker. The thought of smoking first disrupted my concentration. Moving out of my chair and walking to the nearest designated smoking area broke the chain of thoughts. Finally, the flow of creative ideas was decimated after I reached the designated smoking area and smoked the cigarette while engaging in a little chit-chat with a smoking buddy or flipping through the endless stream of mostly useless information on the internet. With fifteen or twenty smoking breaks a day, it took much longer for me to pull the ideas together to create something substantial. I never had long periods of uninterrupted work.

I have also thought about why I was stupefied by a cigarette, not to realize that it was destroying my productivity. I considered the following three possibilities:

1. Smoking altered my brain's biochemistry to stupefy me.

2. Smoking caused physical brain damage to stupefy me.

3. I falsely believed that smoking made me more productive to justify my habit just the way I invented stressors.

The only way for me to assess the effect of smoking on my creativity or productivity is by comparing them to a time when I was a nonsmoker. Like many of you, I started smoking in my adolescent years when being creative or productive in the professional context did not even find a spot on my priority list (if such a list did exist). So how could I possibly know if smoking made me creative or productive if I was already a smoker when these words started to gain relevance in my life? I could not; I wrongly believed that smoking made me productive because that was the only way I knew how to function as an adult. I did not know what it was like to focus for long periods and the full extent of my productivity. If you started smoking at an early age, the same fallacy has corrupted all of your experiences after smoking that first cigarette.

"I cannot drink [alcohol] without cigarettes." You have never enjoyed a drink without smoking.

"I cannot think [about life problems] without cigarettes." You never have. You became aware of the intricacies of navigating the social fabric as an adult, and only after you took up smoking.

"I cannot speak on the phone without a cigarette." I am sure that you were not speaking on the phone as a part of your job when you were fifteen. Saying hi to your grandma is inherently different from negotiating bulk-order pricing with a client.

"I cannot participate in an intellectual discussion." Again, what intellectual discussion were you engaged in when you picked up the habit of smoking? For me, it was discussing new strategies and cheat codes for Counter-Strike, a popular computer game of the day.

You get the point; this is similar to the ever-entertaining Windows vs. macOS debate. Most consumers have not used the other and yet would swear about how their choice of computer operating system is superior. How do users of a MacBook know that it is, in fact, better than a Windows PC if they have never used the latter? Just because one is more familiar with a MacBook does not make it superior. Only after users try their hands on a Windows PC they can comment on the superiority of the preferred operating system citing specific reasons. To help you judge the validity of your reasons to smoke, I have provided you with some space at the end of this chapter to list them out. After you compile the list of reasons, ask yourself if you experienced any of the listed items before taking up smoking.

Before quitting, I thought smoking made me creative and productive at work, and this was perhaps the most persuasive justification I used to sustain my smoking habit. Fear of losing creativity and productivity at work if I quit smoking was one of the biggest challenges I faced. As a result, I postponed my quit date several times or fell into the I-will-temporarily-smoke-until-this-project-is-complete trap. But the hard truth is this: *life will never get any simpler than it already is, and there is no such thing as temporary smoking.* As we have seen, just one cigarette initiated an avalanche of changes in your brain that ultimately hijacked your thought processes. Be wary of just one cigarette and temporary cigarettes. They will become a permanent habit before you know it.

After I reread Tolstoy's essay during my introspections, I reviewed my professional life and realized that I had got a lot of work done, but none of my professional accomplishments stood out. There was nothing that I could be proud of. I knew that I was capable of more than what I had achieved until then. I didn't know what was holding me back, but now, I see it. As a smoker, I never had long enough periods of focus and concentration to assimilate my big ideas.

Contrary to my beliefs as a smoker, I was suddenly more creative at work, was generating better scientific ideas, and came up with novel strategies to engage my students (which is a big challenge at Japanese universities) almost immediately after I quit smoking. Since becoming a nonsmoker, I have significantly expanded my research work, published several articles in top journals, and authored four books, all while maintaining a relatively high teaching load and meeting the demands of being a new father. I was also more creative in making plans to ensure financial security and a healthy lifestyle for my family, both of which I had neglected before (I will revisit these ideas in part two).

But this book is all about the scientific evidence. What does science say about the effects of smoking on creativity, productivity, and focus?

There is good evidence to support the notion that nicotine, when administered in pure form (not cigarettes) in clinical tests, produces positive effects on attention and memory well beyond withdrawal relief [87]. Yes, you read that right. The evidence indicates that nicotine makes you more attentive and improves your memory. The internet goes abuzz with stories like these. But this is a classic case of how summarizing scientific evidence without enough context can completely alter our understanding (A lot of nutritional and weight loss information out there also suffer from the same problem).

Let's have a closer look at the evidence for how nicotine can improve your attention and memory.

First, you need to understand the three functional components of attention: alerting, orienting, and executive attention. When a particular thing in your environment, say, a barking dog on the street, attract your attention, your alerting attention is at play. But alerting attention only makes you aware; it is the orienting attention that gets you hooked. If the specific stimulus demands your attention and you continue to direct your attention towards it, orienting attention has taken over. But what if several things are seeking your attention? For example, you are watching the telly, and the phone begins to ring. As you answer the phone, you see that the oily frozen snack that you had put out on the pan is on fire. You can't be doing all three at the same time. This is when your executive attention will step in, block potentially distracting information—in this case, the phone call and the voice of the talk show host on the television—and focus all of your attention towards the pan on fire.

Nicotine has positive effects on the accuracy and response time of alerting attention (only in smokers but not in nonsmokers), does not affect orienting attention (in smokers or nonsmokers), and reliable reports on the effects on executive attention are not available [87].

Further, nicotine improves the accuracy of short-term memory but only of personal experiences [87]. Nicotine does not affect working memory, which is responsible for temporarily holding information available for processing [87]. There is no evidence to suggest any beneficial effects of nicotine on long-term semantic memory that processes ideas and concepts not drawn from personal experiences, prospective memory that reminds you to perform a planned action, arithmetic, reasoning, and complex cognition [87].

The take away is this: nicotine makes you more alert and helps you remember the recent event in your life if you are a smoker but does absolutely nothing for a nonsmoker. This is clear evidence that nicotine by itself does not improve alertness and recent memory; otherwise, nonsmokers should have experienced these benefits as well. Instead, nicotine only alleviates the shortcomings of a smoker's brain. Even then, this cannot be a strong enough motivation to continue smoking. These positive effects of nicotine are only observable immediately after a cigarette. But what does the evidence say about the long-term (ranging from a few days to years) effects of smoking and exposure to nicotine? Just the opposite. Memory and cognition sharply decline in long-term smokers compared to nonsmokers [88-91].

The evidence for the damage caused by smoking to your ability to think and create memories is vast and can fill an entire book. Here, I will do my best to list the known effects of smoking on different aspects of our mental abilities as concisely as possible.

- Young smokers, especially males, have poorer working memory [90, 92]. Quitting can improve your working memory [90, 92, 93].

- Smokers perform worse than nonsmokers on:

  o Sustained attention and information processing speed [94, 95].

  o Receptive and expressive language, oral arithmetic, and auditory-verbal memory [96].

  o Impulse control, planning, and reasoning [90, 95].

  o Cognitive function [fn08] [97, 98].

- Smoking also causes physical damage to the brain, which includes (all relative to nonsmokers):

  o Reduced blood flow to all parts of the brain [99].

  o Loss of neurons and the connections between them in all regions of the brain [99-101].

  o Decrease in the volume of the frontal lobe of the brain, a region that controls movement, speech, and expression of emotions [102]. The frontal lobe also houses the prefrontal cortex, and any damage to the frontal lobe

---

[fn08] Smoking caused cognitive impairment. As defined by The Center for Disease Control, cognitive impairment is when a person has trouble remembering, learning new things, concentrating, or making decisions that affect their everyday life.

will diminish the executive functions of the prefrontal cortex.

o Decrease in the volume **of the cingulate cortex** [102-104], a part of the brain that analyzes instinctive thoughts, identifies mistakes, perceive pain, evaluates your role in the social context, evaluates emotions, and is involved in reward-based learning.

o Lower density of neurons in the thalamus, which is the relay system of the brain and regulates sleep and wakefulness [103, 105].

o Lower density of the cerebellum[102, 105], a part of the hindbrain that is involved in fine movements, balance, posture, muscle memory, attention, and language.

Together, this body of research shows that smoking causes physical abnormalities in multiple brain regions which regulates a variety of functions that include but are not limited to memory, reasoning, emotion, impulsive behavior, learning, identifying errors, perceiving pain, movement, posture, and balance [106]. I am sure that as a smoker you have some of these problems.

There is an easy way out of this mess if you are willing to take it. Most of the physical and biochemical damage to your brain, and therefore, your attention and memory recovers after you quit smoking. But does this leave a permanent imprint on your brain? Is it true that once a smoker always a smoker? The answer is both yes and no. Quitting smoking is like getting out of a bad relationship. Even after years of ending the relationship, you may look back at the disappointing experience, but you never mope about it or get back into another bad relationship just for the thrill of it. Smoking has been a big part of your life—and you will always be aware of it—but this doesn't mean that smoking has to be a big part for the rest of your life. You learn from the experience and grow. I decided to turn my otherwise wasted time, health, and money into a useful resource for other smokers with this book. On a personal but equally important level, I intend to use my insights on the vulnerability of adolescents, social pressure, and self-esteem in teaching my children some life skills when they get older. After all, there is no such thing as a bad experience; it's all just experience.

Allow me to sum up the information presented so far bluntly. After decades of studies, with hundreds of scientific papers, the only beneficial effect of nicotine we know of is that it increases alertness and memory of recent events acutely and only in smokers. Nicotine does not have these effects in nonsmokers, and it only compensates for the damages smoking causes in the first place. On the contrary, the list of harmful effects is virtually endless. Are you willing to pay through your nose for smoking to receive this minuscule benefit of nicotine, the need for which was created by cigarettes in the first place? The risks clearly outweigh the benefits, and to rub it on our (smokers) faces, nonsmokers enjoy these benefits and more for free.

So, this was the story of smoking, attention, and memory. But there certainly must be scientific evidence to show that smoking increases productivity. Zilch! Quite the reverse, there is scientific evidence from multiple countries with different work practices and notions of productivity to show that smoking reduces work productivity, including absenteeism (work time missed) and presenteeism (impairment while at work) [107-111]. Importantly, those who quit smoking achieve the same level of work productivity as never smokers almost immediately after smoking cessation [107, 111].

Even without a medical or biology background, Leo Tolstoy was definitely onto something. The simple truth is this: smokers have managed to damage their brain circuits so severely that they cannot function without a cigarette. But functioning is different from being focused or productive. Any damage to the brain will decrease focus and productivity. Moreover, there is time lost to smoking, masking the smell, inventing excuses to justify the frequent absence from your workstations, and loss of concentration due to the compulsive need to smoke, all of which negatively impact productivity.

If there were even a shred of evidence to suggest that cigarettes increase your focus and productivity, employers would be jumping to provide you with free cigarettes instead of fancy sleep-pods at work. This idea is not farfetched, and there is some precedent for this from one of the world's largest employers: The United States military. Soldiers and sailors received cigarettes as part of the K-rations and C-rations during the second world war to deal with the psychological stresses of war [112]. In recent decades the military has been actively discouraging smoking among personnel after the detrimental impact of smoking became evident in "combat readiness" and increased risk of injuries [113-115].

Reason to smoke #3: "I will lose my friends."

Smokers invent stressors and the arguments to support attentiveness, creativity, and productivity to justify our smoking habit. But that's not all that they invent; smokers also invent friends.

Smoking is perceived to facilitate social interaction, and smokers have an endless stream of friends that we make in our regular smoking spots. Smokers hang out with other smokers more often than nonsmokers outside of professional interactions. There are smoking buddies at work, the gym, or your favorite coffee shop. These are people you would never know if it wasn't for the habit of smoking you have in common. Because of the time spend with other smokers, and that we have boarded a sinking ship together by choice, we regard them as friends. But the fact remains that smoking buddies are acquaintances at best and only a handful become lifelong friends. We hardly share any emotional relationship with most of our smoking buddies. Nevertheless, smoking buddies have become an essential part of our social circles through years of smoking, and it is tough to let go.

Unfortunately (or fortunately, depending on your point of view), we crave deep emotional relationships, and the shallow relationships with our smoking buddies doesn't quite cut the mustard. How do we fill our needs? That's right, by inventing imaginary friends who provide us with an emotional fix.

Almost all smokers I know have imaginary friends. These friends are so secretive that some smokers may not even be aware of their imaginary friends. During my honest introspection, I realized that it is relatively easy to overcome other barriers to living a smoke-free life, but letting go of my imaginary friends was hard. I enjoyed spending time with my imaginary friends. My imaginary friends had stuck with me through thick and thin. I miss them even today, years after I quit smoking for good. I did not want to let them go until I realized the stupidity of this line of thinking of a smoker's brain. Before you think I have lost my mind and am ranting nonsense, let me explain our imaginary friend problem with some intimate detail.

It took me very long to realize my imaginary friend problem because the problem emerged from a deep-rooted behavioral issue. I was always very fussy about things and people. I had a tiny group of friends in my pre-teenage years. This behavior continued into adolescence. Overtime our priorities diversify, and my friends were not always available on-demand. I learned to cope with different emotions on my own instead of following the natural human instinct of falling back on people. Instead of sharing my happiness and sadness with others, I learned to keep it all within me. It was a revelation of sorts when I lit the first cigarette. I had met the perfect friend that does not talk, think, judge, or demand commitments.

The two most common emotions humans share are sadness and joy. I quickly learned to depend on cigarettes at the low moments of my life. These cigarettes were my de-stressor cigarette. I could spend a few minutes of solitude with my de-stressor cigarette, hoping all the problems in life that were making me sad would simply wash away. During periods of joy or having achieved a significant milestone, I reached for a cigarette instead of reaching out to a friend. Over time this cigarette became an essential part of celebratory or joyous moments. Smokers call this the victory cigarette (or sometimes victory smoke). Almost all smokers I know have at least these two cigarette characters. I have had and heard of several other cigarette characters over the years: the thinking cigarette, the special occasion cigarette, the enjoying the view cigarette, the communication cigarette, and the beer companion cigarette. Never once do we question the irrationality of this concept. But hey, if we were rational about smoking, we wouldn't have lit up the first one.

If the fear of losing your imaginary friends is a reason to smoke your tar filled cigarettes, here is an advice: make friends with the lamppost near your favorite smoking area. Just like a cigarette, it is inanimate, does not talk, think, judge, or demand commitments. Even better, it is always there, and you can find another one if you move to a different city or go on a vacation. It also does not cost you money or kill you. Every time you feel sad or achieve something great, sit next to the lamppost and enjoy the view. How is the emotional feeling offered by the lamppost any different from smoking?

Smoking cannot be a solution to your friend problem; it is the cause of your friend problem. You have structured your life around smoking for so long that the odds are in favor of your new friend being a smoker. Think about it this way: only one-fifth of the world's adult population were smokers in 2016. As a smoker, you are eliminating the chance to become friends with 80 percent of the world's adult population. Statistically speaking, the chances of finding your life partner, business partner, or a lifelong friend among nonsmokers is four times higher. With smoking now accepted as anti-social behavior in all quarters, smokers are depriving themselves of a vibrant social circle that we so naturally crave.

Reason to smoke #4: "I am addicted to nicotine."

Stress relief is the number one reason why people want to smoke cigarettes, but nicotine addiction takes the prime spot among the reasons why they can't quit. Most smokers think that they are addicted to nicotine and cannot escape from the clutches of this monster. I have already shown you the evidence that smokers are addicted to cigarettes but not necessarily to nicotine. There is a little more myth-busting to be done.

The idea that nicotine causes addiction stems from the fact that smoking causes the release of large amounts of dopamine in the brain [116, 117]. Dopamine is a small molecule, secreted by the cells of your body, that helps nerve cells communicate with each other and is famously known to activate the reward pathway in the brain. Dopamine is essential for the normal functioning of the brain, and the lack of dopamine leads to conditions such as Parkinson's disease. Small amounts of dopamine are always released to maintain healthy brain functions.

The relationship between smoking and dopamine is complicated and goes somewhat like this. Nicotine in cigarettes triggers a release of large amounts of dopamine from nerve cells to produce a pleasurable and rewarding experience [118]. Usually, the brain handles a one-time massive release of dopamine without any problems. But the repeated large release of dopamine with frequent smoking causes excessive stimulation of other nerve cells. The brain copes with this hyperactivity by reducing the number of sites on the nerve cells were dopamine can bind [fn9] [118]. Now even with a large amount of dopamine flooding the brain of a regular smoker, the reduced number of binding sites does not allow all of the dopamine to stimulate the brain and therefore maintain normal brain activity [118]. In other words, this adaptation prevents your brain from getting fried every time you smoke. But, this adaptation boomerangs when the smoker is not smoking. The natural release of dopamine in between cigarettes is no longer sufficient to produce normal brain activity due to the decrease in the number of dopamine binding sites. As a result, the smoker experiences withdrawal symptoms such as depressed mood and will crave for the next cigarette. This is a load of baloney!

A recent study published in the journal *Psychopharmacology* showed that smoking does not change the number of binding sites of dopamine; instead, the activity of a protein (unostentatiously called the dopamine transporter) that ferries dopamine in and out of the cell changes [119]. There is also a considerable body of evidence to show that smoking suppresses an enzyme called monoamine oxidase, which is responsible for breaking down dopamine in the cells [120]. As a result, dopamine levels are higher in the brain of a smoker. Further evidence suggests that the non-nicotinic components produce this suppression of monoamine oxidase and, therefore, higher levels of dopamine [120, 121] (more proof against the nicotine-addiction myth). Interestingly, the activity of monoamine oxidase

---

[fn9] Dopamine, like most neurotransmitters and hormones, binds to specific proteins on the cell surface called receptors. Once dopamine binds to its receptor, the receptor produces electrical activity inside the cell that we commonly refer to as a nerve signal.

increases by 20 percent after three days, and by about 50 percent after a month of quitting smoking [122].

Moreover, cigarettes are not exclusive trigger for the release of dopamine. Triggers such as food, sex, candies, chocolate, music, good grades, and exercise can cause the release of large amounts of dopamine and therefore produce a rewarding and pleasurable experience. All habits, especially the ones that have a cue and a learned response, when performed exactly as learned, cause a release of dopamine [123-125]. Smoking causes a release of dopamine because it is a learned habit that is performed in response to particular cues such as stress, just like eating food when hungry.

There are some elegant scientific studies with denicotinized cigarettes, which I mentioned while discussing the issue of addiction in earlier chapters, that dispels the nicotine-dopamine-addiction myth further. Dopamine release was observed in study subjects smoking both ordinary and denicotinized cigarettes [19, 20]. Importantly, there is a plethora of evidence to show that both types of cigarettes reduce cravings and produce the pleasurable experience often attributed to smoking [18-25]. How can denicotinized cigarettes induce all the rewarding, satisfying, and pleasurable sensation typically associated with regular cigarettes if nicotine is responsible for these effects? The evidence is loud and clear no matter how you look at it: it is not nicotine! Only when smokers knew beforehand if the cigarettes contained nicotine or not, they found nicotine-containing cigarette more satisfying or pleasurable [26]. It appears as if smokers desperately want nicotine to produce a rewarding and pleasurable effect.

So why do smokers feel they are addicted to cigarettes? It is a strong habit that is made even stronger by stereotyping. Smoking is subjected to intense stereotyping, often self-inflicted by smokers. A stereotypic image of a typical smoker is as follows. A smoker needs a cigarette first thing in the morning. Otherwise, they will be unbearably grumpy. Smokers always have a pack of cigarettes and lighter with them and panic strikes if they run out of it in the evening. They go driving around town to find a gas station where they can buy the stock to last them the night. And my favorite: smokers cannot function without cigarettes and will suffer unbearable withdrawal symptoms if they quit smoking.

There are two ways to look at the stereotype. First, have you, as a smoker, tried to see what happens if you deliberately do not smoke your morning cigarettes or go through the night with an empty pack of cigarettes? Importantly, what withdrawal symptoms will you experience, and how severe will they be? Since we have unique histories and motivations, our answers to each of the questions above will also be different. But most of us don't know the answer to any of these questions out of our first-hand experience. We believe that depriving ourselves of cigarettes will cause mayhem because that is the prevailing stereotype of a smoker.

But even if I agree for the sake of this argument that you are strongly addicted to nicotine and abstaining from smoking will cause intense agitation, I am sure the other view of the stereotype will help. The stereotype of a typical smoker that I described above is not at all unique to smoking. You need food in the morning, you will experience unbearable hunger if you withdraw from food, and you tend to crave food several times throughout the day. If you have the habit of stepping into the shower before breakfast and don't do it on a particular day, you will feel dirty and stale the entire day. Most of us use a minty toothpaste. If for some reason your toothpaste does not taste minty, you will have an unsavory taste in your mouth all day. Are you addicted to food, shower, or your minty toothpaste? Of course not! Since smoking, eating and cleaning your mouth with a mint-flavored toothpaste are motivated by avoiding an unfavorable situation (stress, hunger, and bad breath), they are all strong habits. And yet, you single out smoking and think that letting go of cigarettes will unleash hell; why? That's because smokers, doctors, celebrities, and governments have convinced you over the past four decades that smoking (ahem, nicotine) is addictive and that escape is impossible without your fair share of suffering. You don't think the same way about food, shower, or mint-flavored toothpaste as such a stereotypic image does not exist for these daily activities.

These are the facts:

- You have developed a strong habit of smoking.

- Since there is little evidence for the chemical basis of addiction to cigarettes, your withdrawal symptoms will be largely behavioral, which are typically very mild and brief.

I will not deny that some people experience terrible withdrawal symptoms. If you believe that you are addicted, then the withdrawal symptoms can be more severe. This is the classical nocebo effect [126], a cousin of the famous placebo effect. The placebo effect is when patients recover from their ailment with a sugar pill after researchers intentionally misled them into believing that they were receiving a fancy new drug. Nocebo effect is the placebo effect working negatively. If the patients are treated with the same sugar pill as if it was the real deal, but this time the researcher convince them that the "drug" may produce some negative side effects, guess what, those terrible side effects will manifest in real life even with a sugar pill. Placebo and nocebo effects are the best scientifically documented cases of the power of mind over medicine.

Cigarettes have a placebo effect when you smoke and have a nocebo effect when you quit. Your mind produces physiological effects because you believe, for whatever reasons, that smoking does a lot of good for you (relaxing, better concentration and focus, pleasurable, and rewarding). Similarly, you have come to believe that depriving yourself of cigarettes will create havoc, and these beliefs will manifest as restlessness, irritability, agitation, anger, low mood, and anxiety as a part of the nocebo effect.

When I quit smoking, the only withdrawal symptom I experienced was restlessness. My past quit attempts were probably far more difficult because I believed that I was addicted and was sure to suffer terrible withdrawal pangs upon quitting. I have contemplated on the difference between my final and earlier unsuccessful quit attempts for weeks. I ruled out motivation as a factor as I had stronger motives during past quit attempts (embarrassment, recurrent miscarriages, losing my dearest uncle to smoking-induced throat cancer, and debt of college education). I was able to pin down two key differences in my successful and unsuccessful quit attempts. In the past, I believed that I was addicted to nicotine despite knowing that the evidence to support nicotine addiction is dismal at best. I suppose I failed to see this evidence beyond the realms of journal articles. The second difference was how I used willpower in my quit attempts. I was more strategic about the use of willpower in the final quit attempt and, importantly, did not rely solely on willpower to quit. I will revisit the science of willpower in a later chapter on *Experimentation*. In short, I used honest introspection and scientific evidence to break down layers of misconceptions and stereotypes to see smoking for what it truly is: a bad habit which is much easier to break than we think.

Reason to smoke #5: "I have an addictive personality."

There is no such thing as an addictive personality. Have you heard a drug addict or any other person ever use the phrase addictive personality? Probably not. But this phrase commonly comes up among smokers. This is yet another thing smoker conjure to justify their smoking behavior. Unfortunately, in this case, the media popularized addictive personality to such an extent (23,700,000 hits on Google!) that it slowly wiggled its way into science. So that we are clear on this, personality traits exist—five of them to be precise—and addictive personality is not one of them. It is also true that some of the five personality traits can influence smoking behavior. Below, I have provided an overview of the five personality traits and how they affect smoking behavior.

The five-factor model (also called the Big Five), initially conceptualized by eminent personality psychologists Paul Costa and Robert McCrae in the late '80s, divide personality traits into five broad domains as follows:

1. *Extraversion:* Describes a person's inclination to seek stimulation from the outside world, especially in the form of attention from other people. Extraverts are friendly, talkative, and often forward in social situations.

2. *Neuroticism:* Describes a person's tendency to experience negative emotions, including fear, sadness, anxiety, guilt, and shame. People with high neuroticism scores are more fearful, anxious, and tend to overthink or exaggerate the severity of

their problems. Neuroticism can result in a person coping less successfully with inconveniences of life [fn10].

3. *Agreeableness:* Describes a person's tendency to put the need of others ahead of their own and to cooperate rather than compete with others. Such people are generous, friendly, cooperative, and considered more likable by their peers and colleagues.

4. *Conscientiousness:* Describes a person's awareness of their actions and the consequences of their behavior. People with higher conscientiousness are goal-oriented and exercise self-discipline to pursue their goals.

5. *Openness to experience:* Describes a person's tendency to think in abstract, complex ways and try new experiences.

There is good scientific evidence to indicate that people with certain personality traits may be more inclined to take up smoking and have a higher chance of relapse. The most extensive study of its kind that included data from nearly eighty thousand men and women from Australia, Germany, the United Kingdom, and the United States show that smokers score higher on extraversion and neuroticism [127]. Smokers also score lower on conscientiousness [127]. Of the big five domains, neuroticism strongly predicts the lower likelihood of quitting and a higher chance of relapse [127]. None of this should come as a surprise to any smoker. But is your fate sealed if you score higher on any of these personality traits? Of course not. Higher extraversion and neuroticism with lower conscientiousness makes such a person more vulnerable but does not confer a permanent smoking status [fn11].

Fortunately, you are not stuck with the same personality traits forever. All the Big Five domains change through different stages of your life. More recent research from Costa and McCrae showed that young people below

---

[fn10] The present-day definition of neurotic is more inclined towards a person with some sort of mental illness than a person who has an exaggerated experience of negative emotion. In the context of personality traits and this book, the latter definition is intended.

[fn11] You can get your score for the Big Five dimensions of personality on this website: https://www.outofservice.com/bigfive/

twenty-nine years of age are less agreeable and conscientious, and these traits increase after the age of thirty [128]. Neuroticism and extroversion also begin to decline around the age of thirty [128]. Further, openness peaks around the age of nineteen and sharply drops after that [128].

All smokers should be able to relate to these findings in the context of their smoking timeline. They are highly open to trying new things (read: cigarettes) before the age of nineteen, continue to smoke in their 20s when they are least likely to be agreeable and conscientious and more likely to score higher on neuroticism and extroversion. After the age of thirty, when agreeable and conscientious begin to increase, and neuroticism and extroversion start to decrease, many smokers seek to quit smoking. But because of the intense stereotyping and misinformation as discuss thus far in this book, they fail and remain smokers until the insidious cigarette finally kills them.

If you are thirty years or older, your biological clock is already altering your personality into one that favors quitting smoking. Instead of using personality as a justification for smoking, you will reap great benefits if you go with the flow of nature and use your changing personality to quit smoking. Everything is working in your favor, but are you? Ask yourself this question when the next urge to smoke hits and after you are done contemplating about cigarettes and hungry lions.

There is one more reason (reason #6 if you like) that smokers frequently use to justify smoking. It is that *"smoking helps me wake up in the morning."* Unlike the five reasons presented in this chapter, this sixth reason is real and genuine but does not deserve lengthy deliberations. Virtually anything that kills you will wake you up, and cigarettes are no exceptions. Cigarettes irritate the linings of mouth, throat, and lungs (which are very dry in the morning), increase heart rate, raise blood pressure, and pumps a concoction of seven thousand chemicals that is more toxic than the contents of a cesspit into your brain. I sure do hope this wakes you up.

I hope that you can now see smoking beyond the misinformation and stereotype. Because if you do, you will see that the real reason you smoke is the fear of missing out. Fear of missing or FOMO is a psychological phenomenon that leads consumers to make impulsive purchases during a made-up holiday sale, fearing they might miss out on the deal of a lifetime. Similarly, you smoke, fearing you might miss out on the experience it offers. You smoke, unsure if you will be able to handle the stresses of life or enjoy parties without cigarettes. And this fear is understandable. All your experiences as an adult have been with a cigarette. You have never handled a stressful situation or gone out for celebratory drinks as a non-smoking adult.

In reality, you will not miss out on anything if you quit. You have now seen the evidence that smoking does not boost your self-esteem, improve your social status, make you creative or productive, and relieve your stress. Instead, the opposite is true; smoking makes you anti-social, destroys your ability to concentrate, causes stress, and damages your self-esteem. Most importantly, you will be missing out on the time with your loved ones and things that bring you joy if you continue to smoke. The list of gains that you can enjoy by quitting smoking is endless.

I expect many of you are reading this with a firm commitment to quit. At the very least, I hope that you now see how irrational and logic-defying smoking truly is. If this analysis of how you fell into this trap of smoking wasn't enough for you to muster the courage to let it go, don't worry. Just the way I showed you how you fell into the trap, I will help you see the way out of the damning habit in part two of this book.

Chapter Summary

✓ Cigarettes stupefy its user into believing that it relieves their stress, increases concentration, makes them creative or productive, and it is a friend in need.

✓ The reverse is true: smoking causes stress, destroys focus and creative thinking, decreases productivity, and limits one's social circle.

✓ You are only addicted to nicotine if you think you are and will have withdrawal symptom if you think you will.

✓ If you are over thirty years of age, the natural changes in your personality traits favor quitting smoking.

Part Two

The Process of Quitting

"Start by doing what's necessary; then do what's possible; and suddenly you are doing the impossible."

-Saint Francis of Assisi.

The cycle of quitting and relapse

There is this tremendous body of knowledge in the world of academia where extraordinary numbers of incredibly thoughtful people have taken the time to examine on a really profound level the way we live our lives and who we are and where we've been. That brilliant learning sometimes gets trapped in academia and never sees the light of day.

-Malcolm Gladwell, bestselling author of "Outliers"

The most likely outcome of any quit attempt is a relapse. In a way, smokers are locked in a vicious cycle of quitting and relapse. The repeated failure to quit is rarely because of the inadequacy of motivation, determination, or the plethora of methods out there that claim to help you quit. It is because smokers do not understand the process of quitting. I will be lying if I tell you that quitting is a one-step process. Changing any behavior rarely has the luxury of an easy-fix escape button.

I am not holier-than-thou. I spend most of the five years trying to quit smoking, equating the process of quitting to getting over a hump. I believed, despite my medical knowledge, that if I can go without a cigarette for twenty-four hours, then three days, then five days, then a week, weeks will turn into months and months into years, and I will live happily ever after. I thought that the act of quitting followed by counting hours, days, weeks, and years is somehow enough to quit.

This changed in my final quit attempt. Like my friend Li said, quitting smoking is indeed very easy, but staying quit is hard. I put more effort into staying quit than towards the act of smoking my last cigarette. We need to hammer away elements of our smoking habit, one stroke at a time—just like Masamune, the legendary 13th-Century Japanese Swordsmith hammering each layer of steel to create some of the greatest *Katanas* in Japan.

But fortunately, we do not have to toil in hot furnaces over months to create hardened nonsmokers as strong as Masamune's famous swords. In part one, we have removed all the stereotyping and misinformation surrounding smoking. I hope that you are now convinced beyond a reasonable doubt that smoking is a behavioral issue and not nicotine addiction. All that is left to do is understand the various stages of quitting and relapse and how to escape from this cycle.

The science of quitting smoking is very well developed, but it has remained within the realms of scientific experiments. In this chapter, I will break down the science for you so that you can reap the benefits of the research work that you paid for through your taxes. Let me re-emphasize that I cannot give you a method to quit smoking. Every smoker is unique and must individually develop a quit smoking plan based on their needs and circumstances. I can only present the guiding principles with examples from my experiences. It is up to you to use this information and develop a personalized quit method suited to your situation.

We are still learning about how some smokers successfully quit smoking. But this does not mean we do not know enough already. In the early '80s, two American psychologists James Prochaska and Carlo DiClemente, published their landmark papers *"Trans-Theoretical Therapy - Toward A More Integrative Model of Change"* and *"Stages and Processes of Self-Change of Smoking: Toward An Integrative Model of Change"* [129, 130]. In these papers, Prochaska and DiClemente presented what has now come to be known as the *Transtheoretical Model of Change*. They theorized that the process of quitting has six stages, namely, pre-contemplation,

contemplation, determination, action, maintenance, and relapse. All current and former smokers can relate to these stages. People who relapse may try to quit again by entering the pre-contemplation stage. Smokers will have to permanently escape from this cycle of quitting and relapse to become nonsmokers again.

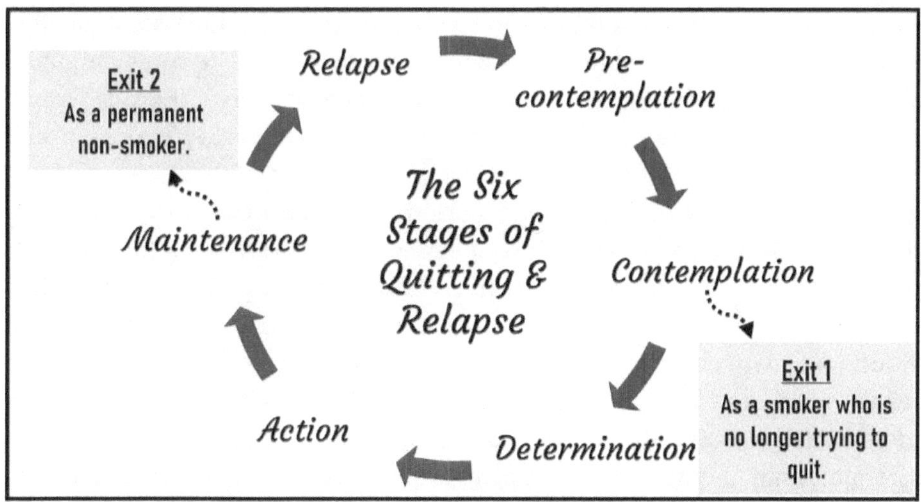

When smokers first consider the need to quit smoking, they rarely have enough determination to quit and may not even have any immediate intention to quit. The smoker has merely found a motivation that provoked the thought of quitting. Earlier I mentioned that motivation alone rarely leads to action, but it is the essential first step of any behavioral change. This is the pre-contemplation stage. Many of you have probably been in the pre-contemplation stage several times. Although this stage seems to have no immediate impact on your smoking behavior, it is a step in the right direction. Before the pre-contemplation stage, the brain saw smoking as a solution to your life's problems, but now it recognizes smoking as a problem for the first time.

The pre-contemplation stage can last anywhere between a few days to years. But once that whimsical thought registers smoking as a problem, the smoker's brain will be on a constant lookout for an opportunity to address the problem. When the smoker realizes that smoking is negatively affecting their health, relationships, time, and money, the brain will see this as an opportunity to build the determination to quit smoking. The smoker then enters the contemplation stage and will seek more information about the harms of smoking, quit smoking strategies, and may even experiment with some of the strategies they discover.

About two-thirds of the smokers who transition from the pre-contemplation to the contemplation stage successfully quit smoking [131]. Sadly, the remaining one-third abandon their plan to quit smoking altogether at this stage and escape the six-cycle stage (Exit 1). Many smokers who exit the cycle at the contemplation stage may make a grand re-entrance a few months later into the pre-contemplation stage, trying to quit again. The lack of determination or superficial ideas that we mistakenly take as motivations are the most common reasons for failing at the contemplation stage. Remember that smoking is an incredibly emotional process. Most smokers pick up their first cigarette in full emotional maturity and often with an underlying emotional reason. As a result, smokers form an emotional bond with cigarettes. Therefore, it is impossible to quit unless the motivations for quitting are emotionally stronger than the act of smoking. It is precisely for this reason that the second part of this book becomes necessary. You will have to learn to supercharge your motivations by building determination to sustain the efforts toward becoming a permanent nonsmoker. Once you are determined to quit smoking for good, you may set a tentative timeline to quit (after Christmas, new year, the birth of a child, or completion of a major project).

But all smokers who move beyond the contemplation phase, spend some time building up the determination to quit. As I have learned from my failed quit attempts, this step can make or break your goal of becoming a nonsmoker. The difference between having a motivation to quit and building determination was quite a revelation for me that significantly contributed to the success of my final quit attempt. Once I became determined to quit smoking, every cigarette I smoked carried a feeling of guilt with it. The irrationality of my behavior bemused me. I became more aware of the pain and inconvenience that I was subjecting myself to sustain the act of smoking. Carrying cigarettes everywhere I went, constantly looking out for designated smoking areas, and the enormous effort to mask the vile smell of burned tobacco started to become a chore. Some part of me was beginning to evaluate the situation rationally as I mindfully smoked my cigarettes.

Before entering the determination stage, I was mindlessly smoking, often unaware of what I was doing. Every day as a smoker, I experienced two versions of me. I was rational, logical, critical, and deliberate in my every action during my cigarette-free hours. But when I lit up, I was numb. I will not go as far as to say that I was irrational, illogical, non-critical, or non-deliberate. I was completely dazed for the ten minutes between lighting up my cigarette and putting it out against the ashtray. It was as if my brain had completely shut down when I lit the cigarette. The only things I remember about each of my smoking events are lighting the cigarette and extinguishing it. I cannot remember how the smoke felt, how my arms were involuntary taking the cigarette to my mouth, and why I decided to smother the cigarette against the ashtray. Every time I cleaned up the ashtray, I could see that the butts were all of different lengths. There must have been different motivations to put off the cigarette after smoking half, three-quarters, or right down to the filter of the cigarette. No matter how hard I try, I cannot remember any of the details. I was completely unaware.

The only cigarette I remember in my sixteen years of smoking is the very first cigarette. I remember the coughing with the first few puffs, the buzz afterward that lasted for about thirty minutes, and the bitter aftertaste of nicotine and tar. I also remember feeling grown-up, tough, and cool. The punchline of a famous television advert in those days rang true in my head [fn12]: "with a cigarette in my hand, I felt like a man." The fifteen-year-old me had no way of knowing then that the professional training I was about to receive as a medical scientist over the next sixteen years, along with my experience of being a smoker, will uniquely position me to write this book and help a billion other smokers escape from their cages.

[fn12] Ironically, this was a quit smoking advert!

But I digress. Let's return to the determination stage of quitting smoking.

As the smoker moves through the determination stage, the momentum picks up, and when the desire to quit reaches a critical mass, the smoker will quit smoking (the action stage). Some may quit as planned on the scheduled quit day. But for others like me, the moment of absolute liberation arrived without any warning, well ahead of my planned quit day. I was smoking my usual morning cigarette when an overwhelming feeling of frustration engulfed me after four or five puffs into my cigarette. Within the next ten seconds, I intuitively thought, "*what is the point of smoking another one if I have decided to quit,*" and I angrily extinguished the cigarette.

I was angry, very angry, but mostly at myself. I was angry mainly because I continued to smoke for so long despite having all the knowledge in the world (or at least the access and training to understand it) on the harms of smoking and how to quit. Heck, I even taught about this in my classrooms.

I performed all my morning tasks as usual after putting out the final cigarette. I brushed my teeth, took a warm shower, dressed up for work, and ate my breakfast. It was sometime during this thirty-minutes window that I conceived the idea to write this book. I decided then that I would compile all the scientific evidence necessary to help other smokers quit smoking. Still angry at myself, I threw out the ashtray and the lighter and headed out to work. As I pulled my bicycle out of the parking rack, my anger was replaced with an intense feeling of liberation and a strong sense of purpose. I felt like an exuberant youngster again, taking his new bike for a spin.

By the time I reached my office at the university, I had already begun to devise strategies to prevent a relapse. I think I had learned from my last failed attempt and realized that unless I have an army of strategies, I will not be able to fight the urge to smoke in certain situations. I knew that I did not want to smoke ever again, but at the same time, I also realized that the adversary was strong. I spend most of the day creating plans to prevent a relapse (but I recommend that you devote some time to do this planning *before* smoking the final cigarette. Read more about this in the chapter *on*

Experimentation). I was already in the maintenance phase by the end of the day, where the only objective was to maintain my new-found status of a nonsmoker.

Unlike my past quit attempts, I was very composed and cautiously optimistic about staying smoke-free. In the past, I announced every effort to quit smoking to my family and friends (common advice on the internet), but not this time. This time I was honest to myself (and fortunately rational) to know that I had won the battle, but the war wasn't over yet.

I considered the war ongoing because I understood the *Transtheoretical Model of Change* that I am currently describing to you. I taught about this in my courses but had never taken it out of the academic domain into practice. I knew that the maintenance phase had two possible outcomes. First, and the more plausible one, was to relapse and repeat the cycle of quitting and relapse one more time. The other possible outcome and the one I was determined to achieve was to escape this cycle as a permanent nonsmoker (Exit 2). So statistically, I had a fifty-fifty chance of permanently quitting or going through another relapse. Instead of basking in the glory of something that was only half achieved, I spend the next several weeks working to reduce the chance of relapse from 50 percent to zero. I knew that without this, I would forever *try* to quit smoking and repeatedly relapse. I will describe the maintenance strategies that I created to remain smoke-free in later chapters. You may find some useful and others irrelevant to your situation. Nevertheless, I will give you all the options so that you have a variety to choose from.

Prochaska and DiClemente provide further insights into these six stages of quitting smoking. Their research indicated most ex-smokers spend six to twelve months in the maintenance stage. Also, successful quitters take the second exit after going through the entire cycle for about three times. More recent research from Queen's University also showed that successful quitters required three or more attempts before achieving long-term abstinence [fn13] from smoking [132]. Importantly, this study showed that almost 80 percent of those who quit were unaided; that is, they did not

---

[fn13] In this study, successful quitters had abstained for an average of thirteen years.

depend on nicotine replacement therapy or other medications to quit smoking.

In their 1983 paper, Prochaska and DiClemente provided more information on the specific strategies smokers take during different stages of quitting [130]. They categorized nine hundred past and current smokers into five groups as long-term quitters, recent quitters, pre-contemplators, contemplators, and relapsers. The psychologist interviewed the participants every six months for two years to understand how smokers used the following ten processes of change:

1. Consciousness-raising (actively searching for smoking-related information).

2. Self-liberation (reinforcing the belief that it is possible to quit).

3. Social liberation (reinforcing the belief that smoking is an anti-social behavior).

4. Self-reevaluation (feeling disappointed about addiction to cigarettes).

5. Environmental reevaluation (considering the environmental impact of smoking).

6. Counter-conditioning (replacing smoking with another activity to de-stress and relax).

7. Stimulus control (avoiding physical things, places, or situations that serve as a cue to smoking).

8. Reinforcement management (being rewarded for not smoking).

9. Dramatic relief (being influenced by warnings about the health hazards of smoking).

10. Helping relationships (having someone to talk to about their smoking behavior).

As expected, the pre-contemplators reported that they had no intention of quitting smoking in the next year. This group of smokers did not use most of the ten processes. The authors concluded that "the pre-contemplators process less information about smoking, spend less time reevaluating themselves as smokers, experience fewer emotional reactions to the negative aspects of smoking, and do little to shift their attention or their environment away from smoking."

The results were clear for those who actively sought to quit smoking. In the contemplation stage, smokers tried to inform themselves of the harms of smoking and ways to quit smoking. They evaluated their motivations to smoke or quit and disappointments with their addiction as they move into the action stage. Once fully committed to the act of quitting, they experience self-liberation. During and after quitting (the action stage), some quitters sought help from others and tried to reward themselves for not smoking. After they quit, recent and long-term quitters replaced smoking with another activity to de-stress and relax (counter-conditioning) and avoid situations that remind them of smoking (stimulus control).

But the crucial findings of the study were these:

- Recent quitters and relapsers were more likely than long-term quitters to seek support from other people to quit smoking.

- Recent quitters and relapsers were more likely to use self-reevaluation (disappointment with self) and reinforcement management (actively seeking reward) than long-term quitters.

- Relapsers were *as likely* to have used counter-conditioning and stimulus control as recent quitters and long-term quitters.

So how can you use this information to quit smoking? First, you do not have to depend on others to support your efforts to quit smoking (another common idea found in quit smoking blogs and videos). With my experience as a smoker and now a nonsmoker, I agree that it is possible and probably better to quit smoking without seeking support from others. You and you alone are fully aware of the myriad of social, emotional, and lifestyle factors that dictates your smoking behavior. This does not mean that you should not talk to other people about quitting smoking; just don't depend on others for support to quit smoking. It is important to rebuild emotional relationships that have been affected by years of smoking. Moreover, suppressing your emotions can lead to faster depletion of willpower [133, 134]. You may, therefore, have to rely on others for general emotional support so that you can exercise more considerable self-control. But this applies to all facets of life and not uniquely to quit smoking.

Second, a positive outlook is essential, and there is no need to seek a reward after quitting. The fact that you can successfully escape the cycle and enjoy your life as a nonsmoker itself can be the reward. I felt guilty, disappointed, and angry towards the end of my final quit attempt. These negative emotions were replaced with a liberating feeling and a strong sense of purpose soon after smoking my last cigarette. Also, I did not seek any short-term reward of quitting smoking, such as buying a fancy watch or the latest iPhone with the money saved. Instead, I used the act of quitting smoking itself as a reward to fuel positive changes in my life as a nonsmoker.

Finally, a well-planned maintenance phase is essential for making a permanent escape from the cycle of quitting and relapse as a nonsmoker. Although counter-conditioning and stimulus control measures do not necessarily predict your chances of long-term success, they are essential for you to quit smoking [135]. Counter-conditioning and stimulus control techniques fill the enormous void left by smoking. These two processes of change did not determine the success of the quitting in the studies discussed above because most smokers do not consider the feasibility and sustainability of their counter-conditioning and stimulus control strategies. Those who successfully quit smoking rely on these strategies for at least a year or two. Any counter-conditioning and stimulus control strategies that are likely to fizzle out in a few days are as useless as a ropeless skipping rope.

A common counter-conditioning technique is eating convenience food such as potato chips or chocolates, as one of my smoking buddies put it, "to mimic the hand-mouth motion of smoking." This is easy to do and perhaps too easy that nibling on high-calorie food is the leading cause of putting on the extra pounds after quitting smoking. This visibly negative result will pave your way into relapsing. (Read more about preventing weight gain in the penultimate chapter on *Maintenance.*)

Another bad counter-conditioning technique I have seen smokers use is playing smartphone games such as Candy Crush. Smartphone games are easy to lug around and can function as counter-conditioning and stimulus control techniques. They can be used to destress, for example, lying on your couch after work, and distract your mind when the cravings are particularly strong. Although smartphone games are perfect distractions (smartphones in general are), they have several problems. You will eventually get bored with it, and you cannot use them on social occasions. You will not receive the best dad, mom, boyfriend, girlfriend, brother, or sister in the world coffee mug for playing Candy Crush at the birthday party of your loved ones.

You must carefully plan the counter-conditioning and stimulus control strategies so that they are easy to execute, don't have any adverse effects, are context-dependent, and sustainable for at least one year. The only way to know if a strategy is feasible and viable is to try it out before you quit smoking.

The six stages of quitting and relapse proposed by Prochaska and DiClemente warrants some revision for those who are ready to quit permanently. I am sure that you have no intention of relapsing, and therefore we can look at the six stages as a linear process (instead of a cycle) that starts with pre-contemplation followed by contemplation, determination, action, maintenance and culminating in the permanent escape. I want to add another stage, the experimentation stage, that Prochaska and DiClemente didn't include in the original model. The experimentation stage will give you the time to create, test, and refine your counter-conditioning and stimulus control strategies before smoking the final cigarette. This will ensure that your strategies to remain smoke-free are easy and exciting enough to perform for several months after you quit smoking.

These revisions to the original Prochaska and DiClemente model give us the seven stages: pre-contemplation, contemplation, determination, experimentation, action, maintenance, and permanent escape that all smokers must go through to become permanent nonsmokers. Since you are reading this book and have read this far, I think it is safe to assume that you have gone past the pre-contemplation and contemplation stages. I will individually address the remaining five stages in the subsequent chapters.

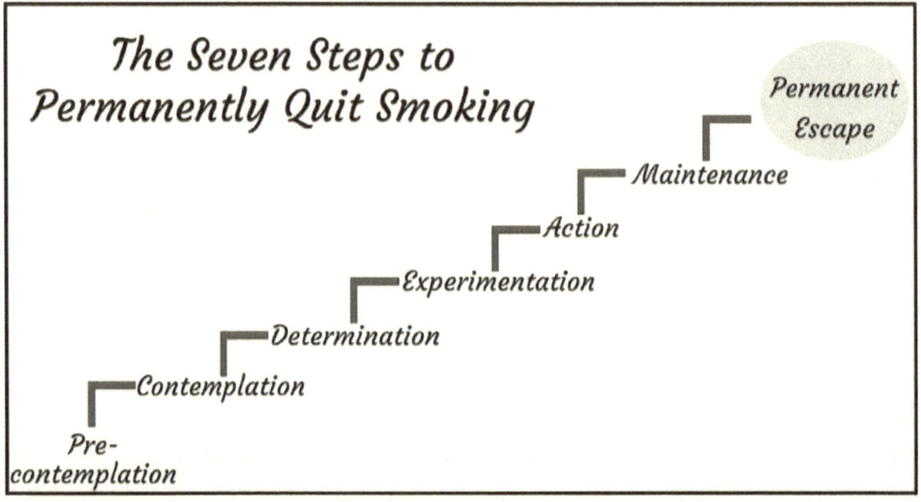

Chapter Summary

✓ Smokers are trapped in the cycle of quitting and relapse.

✓ One can become a non-smoker by permanently escaping from the cycle.

✓ Building determination and strategies to remain a nonsmoker after quitting are crucial.

✓ It is essential to devise, test, and refine your counter-conditioning and stimulus control strategies to ensure that they are easy to perform and sustainable.

Determination: Understand the economics of smoking

*Desire is the key to motivation, but it's determination
and commitment to an unrelenting pursuit of your goal
- a commitment to excellence - that will enable you to
attain the success you seek.*

-Mario Andretti, racing legend

Motivation alone is not enough for you to quit smoking. Smokers who quit due to pregnancy provide an excellent demonstration of this fact. Pregnancy is one of the best motivators to quit smoking. Most smokers, men and women alike, know the harms of smoking on the fetus, but only about 40 percent quit smoking when they become pregnant [136-139]. Moreover, half of them relapse soon after childbirth despite having a strong motivation (breastfeeding, child-rearing, and being a good role model [fn14]) to remain quit [136, 139, 140].

Necessary as they may be, superficial reasons such as "its good for me," "I don't want to die early," or "I want to save some money" or are not well thought out and are knee-jerk reactions to a health scare or a financial tight spot. They are as impulsive as smoking itself. How much money do

---

[fn14] New fathers have at least two of the three motivators (child-rearing and remodeling), and yet this fails to motivate them sufficiently to quit smoking.

you expect to save by quitting smoking? How exactly is smoking affecting your health, and what sort of recovery do you expect? How will you handle stress post-quitting? How will you avoid weight gain? What will you do if an urge to smoke suddenly strikes? These are powerful questions and without answers can derail any quit attempts.

It will help to recall from the first chapter that determination is the process of building an *I-will-succeed-no-matter-what* attitude. Let's be realistic: you will succeed "no matter what" only if you can deal with anything life throws at you. Pure grit and willpower partly support this attitude. While both are indispensable in your quit attempt, they cannot be wholly relied upon (more on willpower in the next chapter). Anticipating difficult and vulnerable circumstances before smoking the final cigarette will make the quit smoking plan staunch and more likely to succeed. Thus, you must think of building determination as an act of reasoning and experimentation to solve potential problems or remove obstacles in your journey towards becoming a happy nonsmoker.

The primary motivators of successful quitters include all the usual suspects—money, physical fitness, being a good role model for children, pregnancy, insistence from partner or family, and health reasons (current and potential future conditions) [56, 141, 142]. All seasoned smokers have, at one time or another, had these motivations. But these strong motivations manifests into successful quit attempts in only a hand full of smokers. The reason—you got it—is the lack of determination. You must provide foundational support to your motivations by building determination. We will be doing just that in this chapter. I will help you create a logical and emotional foundation to quit so that your motivation sustains your efforts until you make the permanent exit from the cycle of quitting and relapse.

In part one of this book, we saw how smoking does nothing *FOR* you—it does not solve your problems, help you concentrate, enhance your creativity, or make you look cool; this does not mean smoking does nothing *TO* you. Smoking robs you of your money, health, and time. But exactly how much does the habit of smoking chew into? Your quest to build determination begins with this question.

Something you should understand about motivation and determination is that they work best if the result is immediately observable. For example, you are more likely to stick to a workout routine that makes you lose a kilogram every week. But if weight loss feels like the nineteen-hour non-stop between Newark and Singapore, you will give up and try the next fad on the list. Unfortunately, money, health, and time all suffer from the same problem—the results are not immediately observable. But can we make the small daily gains of money, health, and time as a result of quitting observable? For this, we will be relying on the wisdom of management guru Peter Drucker. In his 1954 classic *The Practice of Management*, Drucker gave us the catchphrase "What gets measured, gets managed," which has been repeated so many times by business speakers that it has almost become a cliché. The concept, however, is as relevant today as it was sixty-four years ago.

Moreover, 21st-century technology has made it possible to cheaply and easily measure almost anything. You can track the cost of smoking using a free expense tracker on your smartphone, overall health using a wrist-based fitness tracker, and your performance and promotions at work are good indicators of time and productivity (several smartphone-based trackers are also available to track your time by the minute). But, this is a matter for after you quit smoking, and I will discuss each of these strategies in the next chapter as a part of counter-conditioning and stimulus control strategy. First, we need to establish how much you have had to shell out for smoking over the years.

Like all consumer products, cigarettes are vexed by the Diderot's effect, which describes how "purchasing goods that are deviant to an individual's typical buying behavior can begin a spiraling of consumerism." That was tedious just to type. I unknowingly rediscovered Diderot's effect after my wife and I started living together in 2014. We went out to buy a dining table to replace the small *Kotatsu* (a low Japanese multipurpose table) we had in our apartment. My wife spent hours selecting the table that was of the right size, shape, and color. But that was not the end of it as I had hoped. We then spend another couple of hours selecting a table cloth that went well with the drapes we had purchased the week before. And then we had to buy dinner mats to complement the curtains and the table cloth. But if we had to cover the table anyways, then why did we spend hours picking the perfect table? As a tribute to all those who hate shopping, I decided to call this the *tablecloth syndrome.*

Smokers also suffer from tablecloth syndrome, perhaps more so than others. Smokers are eager to try new products and brands: the new heated not burned electronic cigarettes, fancy pouches to carry all your smoking gadgets, and the latest after-smoke mints. Did you own or desired to own a famous, not-so-cheap, branded lighter with your name engraved on it? Do you use mint-flavored gums, lozenges, or spray to mask the smell of cigarettes? How about coffee? For me, the first cigarette in the morning was unthinkable without a cup of coffee brewed by a professional barista. Or, perhaps portable ashtrays and leather tobacco pouches (if you roll your own) that have become a sort of a fashion trend these days, at least in Japan. Smokers pay for more than just cigarettes making smoking a more expensive habit than they realize. For the sake of simplicity, I refer to the group of items that add value to your smoking experience as *smoking accessories.*

And then there is the indirect cost of smoking. One of the major indirect cost of smoking is your time. Smokers take frequent breaks to satisfy their smoking habit. As a result, they deny the task at hand or the people around them their full attention. If you are trying to hide your smoking behavior at work or home, then there is time lost to stalling with the hope that the smell of cigarettes will dissipate.

To this, add the cost of healthcare. Since most smokers believe that they are somehow immune to smoking-related diseases, let me tackle this issue from another angle. In addition to causing unspeakable damage to your health, smoking robs the health of your loved ones. Smoking during pregnancy can severely affect the physical and mental growth of babies even before they are born and puts them at risk of several diseases including but not limited to obesity, diabetes, heart disease, wheezing, asthma, airway hyper-responsiveness, impaired lung function, and bronchitis after birth [143]. The health of the fetus is also affected by the smoking status of the father before conception. Smoking can cause irreversible damage to the DNA in sperm, causing severe congenital disabilities and miscarriages [144].

Smokers also affect the health of their loved ones by exposing them to secondhand smoke. Several studies have provided consistent evidence for increased risk of asthma, allergic rhinitis, sudden infant death syndrome, low birth weight, decreased head circumference, respiratory infections, otitis media (inflammatory diseases of the middle ear), childhood cancer, hearing loss, and metabolic syndrome in addition to adverse cognitive and behavioral outcomes in children exposed to secondhand smoke [145-147]. Secondhand smoke can also be the cause of lung cancer, asthma, COPD, heart disease, and diabetes for nonsmokers around you [148]. All of these conditions are disabling and expensive to treat.

The first-born daughter of one of my smoking buddies suffered from severe respiratory distress because of exposure to secondhand smoke for which she had to use oxygen masks until the age of four, and the family had to lug around gas cylinders everywhere they went. Although this experience moved my smoking buddy to quit, the little girl had to endure incredible suffering, and I am sure so did the parents.

And if your smoking habit encourages your dependents to take up smoking, as it often does, then you will have to pay for the cost of their health care as well. Besides, there are moral considerations. Putting yourself at risk of serious diseases is your personal choice, but do your loved ones deserve to be put at risk of severe and painful conditions because of your smoking behavior?

As you can see, the cost of smoking is far higher than a pack of cigarettes and includes the cost of smoking accessories, healthcare costs, and time lost to smoking. You may need an accountant to make a detailed estimate of how much smoking is costing you. But we can run some basic calculations on at least the direct cost of smoking to get an idea.

Even if you live in a country like Japan where cigarettes are relatively cheap (~$4 for a pack of twenty), the cost of smoking quickly adds up. The direct cost of smoking is not limited to cigarettes alone and must also include the cost of lighters, minty gums, and coffee. As discussed in the earlier chapters, smokers go to great extends to avoid the negative perception of others towards their smoking habit. James, one of my very close friends, keeps a stock of mint-flavored mouthwash at work. He rinses his mouth after every smoke (about fifteen times a day!) and just before he heads home to his wife and two beautiful daughters (who think that he has quit smoking for three years now). James believes that mouthwash will also prevent the staining of his teeth (it does not—bummer, huh?). But let's say that James is an exception, and we will calculate the basic cost of smoking by only considering the price of cigarettes, mint, and one coffee per day for a smoker I'll call Bob.

Bob started smoking at the age of fifteen but is a relatively light smoker and smokes about ten cigarettes a day on average. He is now thirty years old and has decided to quit smoking. Bob lives in Los Angeles, California, where his favorite brand of cigarettes costs $8 (pack of twenty). But since cigarettes were a lot cheaper when Bob started smoking, let's take the average cost of $5 per pack. Over the past fifteen years, Bob has smoked nearly 55,000 cigarettes that cost him $14,000. Now let's add the cost of mint at a conservative $1 a week and another dollar for a cup of coffee per day to go with the morning cigarette. This adds another $6,000 bringing the total direct cost of smoking to $20,000 over fifteen years. You can take these numbers and easily estimate your direct cost of smoking. If you are a pack-a-day smoker, then the total direct cost comes to $34,000 over fifteen years.

My imaginary friend Bob practically threw away $20,000 over the past fifteen years on a product that provided no benefit whatsoever, other than an illusionary experience of helping deal with the stress. If he had kept the money in the bank, he would have an extra $45,000 assuming the bank offered a 5 percent return on savings. This is the second way by which smoking robs you of your wealth. If Bob had invested the same $20,000 in more profitable financial instruments like stocks and assume that the investment gave a conservative 10 percent return, he would have $71,000 today. But all of this is in the past. Let's calculate how much money Bob stands to lose if he continues to smoke for another fifteen years while maintaining the conservative estimates of $5 per pack of cigarettes, $1 per week for mint, and \$1 per day for coffee. The amount will be a staggering \$360,000 over thirty years of smoking! And remember these are very conservative estimates and the actual cost of smoking will be much higher than these estimates.

Now let's quickly calculate the time Bob lost to smoking. Say Bob needs ten minutes to smoke each of his ten daily cigarettes. That is a total of six hundred hours a year. By this estimate, I spend upwards of twelve hundred hours a year as a pack-a-day smoker. Ironically, I complained about being too busy or not having enough time to follow my passions while showing off my ability to make rings of tobacco smoke with my mouth. This book is the direct result of the time saved by not smoking over the past year alone.

Use the three angels of Kahneman to supercharge your motivations.

I am not even close to being the first person to have calculated the cost of smoking. Many before me have made such calculation, and yet the staggering numbers fail to motivate them enough to quit smoking. I think I first calculated my cost of smoking about eight years ago, but this did not excite me enough then. It was after I read *Thinking, Fast and Slow*, the best-selling book by Nobel Prize-winning psychologist Daniel Kahneman, that the cost of smoking evolved as a significant motivator in my final quit attempt. It took me about a week to read the book, another week to digest the information, and in the third week, I had already quit smoking, and this time for good.

In the book, Kahneman provides evidence from his work and those of others to show how humans think and make choices. He elegantly describes two systems of reasoning. System one is fast, automatic, frequent, emotional, stereotypic, and unconscious. In contrast, system two is slow, effortful, infrequent, logical, calculating, and conscious. These systems of thinking appealed to the smoker in me very strongly as I could relate to them. As a smoker, I was using system one of thinking—smoking is an impulsive, emotional, stereotypic, and unconscious habit, as we have seen in the first part of this book. Somehow, system two, which is a rational but effortful process, was suppressed during smoking.

Consequently, I believed almost anything about smoking—smoking relaxes me, improves my focus and concentration, makes me productive, and in times of need, is a friend to me. At the end of Kahneman's book, I remember thinking that there would be no smokers in the world if system two of thinking were our default state. Unfortunately, it is not; system one is.

The moral is significant: when System 2 is otherwise engaged, we will believe almost anything. System 1 is gullible and biased to believe, System 2 is in charge of doubting and unbelieving, but System 2 is sometimes busy, and often lazy. Indeed, there is evidence that people are more likely to be influenced by empty persuasive messages, such as commercials, when they are tired and depleted.

Excerpt from "Thinking, Fast and Slow" by Daniel Kahneman

The insights I gained from Kahneman's book that helped me turn the cost of smoking as a significant motivator to quit came in the form of three economic principles-*loss aversions, sunk cost fallacy, and framing effect.* I call these principles the *three angels of Kahneman* because the lessons learned from them were nothing short of the word of god. Understanding these principles was essential to get my system two of thinking to work and turn system one against smoking.

As Kahneman explains, for most parts of human evolution, our brain has learned to prioritize avoiding or escaping from threats. Consequently, we have greater motivation to avoid loses that pose a threat than to work toward gains. This behavior is called *loss aversion.* It is a compelling force in virtually every aspect of our decision-making process and is part of system one of thinking.

As a smoker, I always believed that smoking served some useful purpose. It calmed me down in stressful situations. It helped me become more social. It helped me concentrate or that it is a friend. The misinformation and stereotype had convinced me that cigarettes had a lot to offer. I smoked to avert potential losses that would emerge from my inability to deal with stressful events or from lack of productivity at work without a cigarette. In other words, I believed that smoking enabled me to professionally and socially function, and I had a lot to lose if I quit smoking—loss of money, peace of mind, and friends.

If you revisit the three introspection tasks in part one, you will see that we are always trying to avert our losses by smoking. Arguments such as I cannot do this or that without smoking, I become grumpy, and I cannot concentrate all work to avert losses; it is for this reason that smoking is so powerful. As smokers, we feel that smoking helps us prevent significant losses in our lives.

This is a typical system one thinking, and we need to flip this. It is necessary to rewire the brains of smokers to think of smoking as a loss— they will automatically avert the loss. But this cannot be achieved with a campaign poster or a two-minute television advertisement. It needs a more systematic approach. Smokers first need to see that the losses they think smoking is averting are not real losses. From the lessons learned in part one, we now know that smoking does not relieve stress but causes it; it does not improve productivity but damages your creative faculties, and it is an anti-social habit.

I wish there were a better word than insanity. The word does not do enough justice to describe the behavior where you pay for a product with your money, health, and time so that you can become more stress, less productive, and anti-social. Smoking is an expensive habit with no potential upside.

Now let's consider Kahneman's second angel: *the sunk cost fallacy*. We tend to use the faster system one more often than system two. As a result, we do not always make our decisions based on sound reasoning and logic, which are functions of system two. Instead, we make most of our decisions based on emotional appeal. Sunk cost fallacy is when we continue our endeavors despite failure as a result of previously invested resources (time, money, and effort). A classic example of this from Kahneman's work is a gambler who puts in more money to recover her lost bets. The gambler's new bets in no way predict her chances of recovering the lost money. Her chances of winning or losing are the same as before. Still, she puts more cash into gambling to cut her losses in the grand scheme of things. The best thing for this gambler will be to think of the money lost as unrecoverable, retain whatever money she has left, and walk away from the table. Most of you will agree that continuing to gamble to recover the sunk cost is foolish.

As we have seen, smoking is an expensive endeavor. Bob, my imaginary friend, who only smokes ten cigarettes a day, is looking at losing a total of $360,000 if he continues to smoke for the next fifteen years. But it isn't just money he is losing. If Bob's favorite brand of cigarettes contains six milligrams of tar and one-milligram nicotine, which is the average for most cigarette brands, he would have smoked three hundred and thirty grams of tar and fifty-five grams of nicotine over the past fifteen years. If you think these numbers don't look that bad, think again. That is enough nicotine to kill as many as one hundred and ten adults (lethal dose on nicotine varies between 0.5-1 gram). Now you can continue to follow system one and think "it took a lot of effort for your body to like the poisonous smoke, and it would be a shame to throw all that hard work down the tubes." Or, you can engage your system two and move away from the table, cutting all your losses here and now. The 111th person to be saved could be you!

The lessons from sunk cost fallacy have another significant implication. Just like the gambler whose unsuccessful endeavor of the past does not change the outcome of the subsequent bets, your failed quit attempts of the past also do not indicate chances of failure in your future quit attempts. Your chance of successfully quitting does not decrease with repeated failed attempts but remains the same. If you have tried to quit a hundred times and failed, it does not change a thing. Your chances of quitting are still the same as for everybody else.

Kahneman's third angel can be used to explain our smoking behavior like the other two angels, but it also takes us a step closer towards becoming a nonsmoker. We make most of our decisions after evaluating the pros and cons, but we seldom give the same weight to the possible positive and negative outcomes of our choices. This is called *the framing effect* and has startling effects on how people make choices. For example, what would you do if I offered you the following hypothetical choices?

Scenario 1: Participate in a two-kilometer race, and you may win $200 or complete a five-kilometer run and receive $200 instantly. Most will go for the latter option despite longer distance as the reward is guaranteed. In comparison, the two-kilometer race is risky, and most will avoid taking this option.

Scenario 2: There is a 99 out of a 100 chance that you will lose all your money kept in the bank and 1 percent chance that you will quadruple your money. Or, you may choose to invest in a start-up firm where you have a 50 percent chance of losing lose all your money and a 50 percent chance of doubling your money. In such a scenario, most would choose to take a risk with the startup firm despite smaller profit and avoid an almost certain loss with the bank.

Framing effect influences your choices in each of these scenarios, and there are two specific lessons to be learned. First, people tend to avoid risk when information is presented in a positive frame (as in scenario 1). In this case, we prefer sure gain over probable gain. And second, we tend to seek risks when information is presented in a negative frame (as in scenario 2) and prefer probable loss over a definite loss. Clearly, we don't see loss and gain equally and prefer sure gains and probable losses.

Now, consider the following statements from the World Health Organization's *Tobacco fact sheet* of 2019 [49]:

Tobacco kills up to half of its users.

Tobacco kills more than 8 million people each year.

Although these are statements of fact (both presented in the negative frame), they rarely have a sizable impact on smokers. When presented with such facts as a part of tobacco scare tactics, most smokers either ignore the information or think in one of the following ways:

- "Since tobacco kills only half of its users, I only have a 50 percent chance of dying. My uncle Joe smoked two packs a day and lived to ninety years."

- "Tobacco only kills eight million of the billion smokers in the world. My chances of dying due to tobacco are quite low."

As predicted by the framing effect, we prefer probable loss over the definite loss. The smoker might as well take the risk since smoking does not kill every one of its users. Moreover, smoking has many sure gains from a smoker's perspective. When we first took up smoking, we saw it as a pathway to more friends, social acceptance, and better social status. Adult smokers will swear that smoking relieves them of their anxiety and stress, makes them more productive, and that smoking is a friend to them.

This is the problem with the way information is presented in our current strategies to curb smoking—smokers perceive the harms of smoking as probable harm and the benefits of smoking as definite gain. Since we are naturally inclined to choose probable loss over the definite loss and definite gain over probable gain, the scare tactics if anything encourages you to smoke. To a smoker, smoking offers the ideal combination of a definite gain (e.g., smoking *certainly* relieves my stress) and probable loss (e.g., smoking *may* cause cancer)—this is why your urge to smoke increases when you see the information from the doom and gloom campaign or if you have a health scare.

Your current view of smoking is that of numerous sure gains and some probable losses. You need to change this frame to view smoking as a definite loss and probable gain (or view quitting smoking as a sure gain and probable loss). The change of frame will ensure that *not smoking* is an automatic and default action as you will be naturally inclined to avert losses (remember loss aversion works as a part of system one which is automatic).

Most of you may have already changed your frame of view in part one, where I provided the arguments and supporting evidence that leaves little room to doubt the fact that you stand to gain nothing from smoking other than the illusion of stress relief and enjoyment. In this chapter, we have seen that smoking leads to a definite loss of money, health, and time. The new frame of smoking and the realization that the losses can be cut immediately by quitting has already turned your system one against smoking. As long as you see smoking as a losing endeavor with nothing to offer in return—and quitting will bring about positive gains—the process of loss aversion will automatically work to keep cigarettes at bay.

You know that if you wake up one morning with symptoms indicating that you will soon be dead, you will feel more regret because you could have rejected the idea of selling your health without even stopping to consider the price.

Excerpt from "Thinking, Fast and Slow" by Daniel Kahneman.

But like I said before, the gains of quitting smoking must be immediately and continuously observable for loss aversion to work. Of the three definite losses of smoking, money is probably the only one that is immediately observable if you calculate the direct daily, weekly, monthly, or lifetime cost of smoking. If you keep track of how much money you spend on smoking daily, you can see how this habit is hurting your finances in real-time. I strongly recommend that you download and use any of the freely available expense trackers on your smartphone for at least two weeks to see just how much smoking is costing you [fn15]. The figure will surprise you.

If expense tracking does not move you enough, then remind yourself that you are only tracking the direct cost of smoking. Smoking also hits you with a sledgehammer through its indirect costs. Smoking robs you of your health, and the poor health will end up costing money in the form of medical bills. The diseases caused by smoking are in no way cheap to treat.

[fn15] I recommend Money Manager and Mint expense trackers based on my user experience.

Smoking causes virtually all types of heart diseases and cancer, most notably high blood pressure, stroke, heart failure, and lung cancer [149, 150]. Smoking is also a leading cause of COPD, including emphysema and bronchitis, type 2 diabetes, elevated cholesterol, macular degeneration, teeth loss, arthritis, peptic ulcers, and fertility issues in both men and women [151]. If you are overwhelmed by this volume of medical information, you might find some consolation in the fact that this is a concise list of diseases caused by smoking.

So, let's bring together the facts about the cost of smoking. First, you pay to sustain the habit. Second, the cost of supporting this habit prevents your wealth from otherwise growing. And third, when you fall sick as a direct result of smoking, then you pay for it again. Even if you believe that you are somehow immune to the diseases caused by smoking, it is clear that smoking produces significant losses in terms of money, time, productivity, and career growth prospects. To sustain the habit of smoking, the gains must undeniably outweigh the losses. So, what do you stand to gain from smoking? Smoking does not remove the stressor and solve your problems, make you perform better at work or in bed, and increase your social attractiveness. You have everything to lose (literally) and nothing to gain (again, literally!) from smoking.

But you stand to gain a lot from quitting smoking (Are you tired of hearing that yet? I hope not, because I am not even close of getting tired of saying it). Quitting will improve your finance, you will regain your health, and you will have full control over your time. I know that I am trying very hard to sell the benefits of quitting, but it deserves that extra salesmanship. Most of us started smoking before adulthood and have not experienced much of what life has to offer without cigarettes. We don't realize just how productive we can be without our brains being devoured by cigarettes like zombies feasting on human flesh. We don't know what celebrations genuinely feel like without being constantly distracted by the need to smoke cigarettes. We don't know what it feels like to be able to run around the park simply because we can (I enjoy this a lot with my young daughter). And we can barely scratch the surface to fully appreciate the hit our finances take to sustain the filthy and parasitic habit. Everything is a new experience after you quit smoking, and this makes it immensely enjoyable.

Chapter Summary

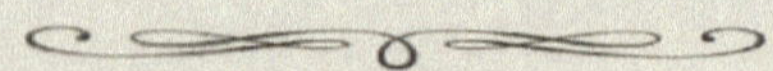

✓ Your reasons to quit smoking must be founded on strong emotion and logic.

✓ You pay for smoking twice: first when you buy cigarettes and second when you see the doctor for your smoking-related illness.

✓ The health of your loved ones is also affected by your smoking behavior.

✓ Smoking in both men and women can lead to miscarriages and congenital disabilities, causing unnecessary suffering of your little ones even before they are born.

✓ Smoking prevents your wealth from growing.

✓ A pack-a-day smoker will lose at least $2,300 and 1,200 hours annually to smoking. Imagine what you could achieve with all that extra time and money.

✓ See smoking for what it really is: an act of definite loss and probable gain.

✓ Your loss of money, health, and time can be prevented immediately by quitting smoking.

✓ You are wired to seek definite gains and avert definite losses. This changed frame will enable not smoking to become an automatic and default action.

Task #4
Why do you want to quit smoking?

✓ List out all your motivations to quit smoking.

✓ Rate the impact of these motivations on your life after you quit smoking. (N= no impact, L= low impact, and H= high impact.)

1. ____________________________________   N — L — H

2. ____________________________________   N — L — H

3. ____________________________________   N — L — H

4. ____________________________________   N — L — H

5. ____________________________________   N — L — H

6. ____________________________________   N — L — H

7. ____________________________________   N — L — H

8. ____________________________________   N — L — H

9. ____________________________________   N — L — H

10. ___________________________________   N — L — H

Task #5
What will you miss the most about smoking after quitting?

✓ List out all the things that you feel will lose or miss out on if you stopped smoking today.

✓ Are you losing too much by quitting? Rate the impact of the loss due to quitting smoking. (N= no impact, L= low impact, and H= high impact.)

1. ____ N   L   H

2. ____ N   L   H

3. ____ N   L   H

4. ____ N   L   H

5. ____ N   L   H

6. ____ N   L   H

7. ____ N   L   H

8. ____ N   L   H

9. ____ N   L   H

10. ____ N   L   H

Experimentation: Create an effective quit smoking plan

There are three principal means of acquiring knowledge... observation of nature, reflection, and experimentation. Observation collects facts; reflection combines them; experimentation verifies the result of that combination.

-Denis Diderot, philosopher and the co-creator of Encyclopédie

The determination stage shows you that the grass is greener on the nonsmoker's side and helps you identify the problems you may face during and after quitting. The experimentation stage will help you solve those problems.

There are four specific issues that any smoker with a serious intention to quit should be concerned about. First, the use of willpower is indispensable in all quit attempts but is as unreliable as a damp matchbox. Second, smokers suffer from tablecloth syndrome, and smoking accessories such as coffee and mint may be as habituating as smoking itself. Third, you have depended on cigarettes to deal with your anxieties and stress; your body is going to want another way to relax. This is where counter-conditioning strategies come in handy. Finally, you have been smoking for so long that you associate many things with smoking, some more strongly than others, and these constant reminders of smoking will lead you into relapse unless you plan to deal with them using stimulus control techniques.

The last two areas of concern become slightly more challenging if you consider the finding from Prochaska and DiClemente's study that relapser, recent quitters, and long-term quitters equally use counter-conditioning and stimulus control techniques. At first glimpse, it seems that counter-conditioning and stimulus control are ineffective in maintaining the new-found status of a nonsmoker. But the important question to ask here is why do relapsers fail despite using counter-conditioning and stimulus control measures?

This question leads us to the most common method of quitting smoking: willpower. Both acts of replacing smoking with another activity and avoiding physical things, places, or situations that remind us of smoking require the use of willpower. Do relapsers have less willpower than long-term quitters? Or were long-term smokers somehow better at using their willpower to quit smoking? In any case, we know that willpower is a limited resource, which I will argue in the next few pages is a true but incomplete assessment.

Smokers have come to associate the act of smoking with smoking accessories, certain places, and times of the day. The habit of smoking has multiple layers like a bulb of onion where cigarettes are merely the outer skin. Underneath lies the habit of smoking with a cup of coffee, at a certain place, at a certain time, and if you observe smokers even facing the same direction while smoking at their favorite spots (my natural inclination was to face east). When you quit smoking, these layers take a big bite out of your willpower.

Moreover, smoking accessories can be triggers for smoking and, therefore, will demand the use of more willpower. We cannot allow these things to take up our limited reserve of willpower, which must be fully available when we have no choice but to resist the urge to smoke.

If you don't offer your body another way to relax, find a way to deal with triggers, and eliminate the non-cigarette ruses of the smoking habit beforehand, guess what, your ship will be sailing solely on willpower. The experimentation stage becomes necessary to avoid such a crisis. In this chapter, you will learn to judiciously use willpower and create and test effective counter-conditioning and stimulus control techniques to help you stay smoke-free after you quit smoking. I will give you the essential elements of good counter-conditioning and stimulus control strategies later in this chapter.

You must test your strategies for staying quit for at least a couple of weeks before smoking the final cigarette. Do not set your quit date until you feel comfortable with your planned strategies and are confident that you can continue to use them for at least a few months or longer if you have to. You don't want to find out that you do not enjoy or lack the time for any of the planned strategies after you stop smoking. For example, you might make plans to hit the gym after you quit smoking only to realize that you don't have enough time or energy on most days to develop and sustain the new habit. This will have a domino effect, and soon you will give up on being a nonsmoker and relapse. You will have to create easy, inexpensive, and sustainable counter-conditioning and stimulus control strategies to replace the habit of smoking and deal with the triggers.

The Science of Willpower

Critics of using willpower to quit smoking point to the fact that willpower is like a battery; it depletes with persistent use. What most of them forget to mention is that willpower is like a rechargeable battery; you can run out of it but also recharge it later. Smokers try to quit using willpower and fail because we have never learned to use it deliberately. I doubt if any of us learned the use of willpower in schools, universities, or through conventional wisdom. We need to look at the science of willpower more deeply to fully appreciate its strengths and weaknesses.

In 1998, social psychologist Roy Baumeister and his colleagues from Case Western Reserve University published their well-known study in which they demonstrated that we have one reserve of willpower and all tasks that requires self-control draw from the same bag [152]. We don't have separate stockpiles of willpower for exerting self-control against sleeping in, binge-watching Netflix, overeating junk food, procrastination, or smoking. Importantly, Baumeister's group showed that willpower is, in fact, a finite resource, which means that the more you exert willpower, the less you have of it [152]. This phenomenon is now famously referred to as the *ego-depletion effect*. Since the first report from Baumeister and his colleagues, over three hundred research studies have confirmed the validity of the ego-depletion effect [153, 154].

Recalling my experience of being a smoker, I couldn't agree more with the ego depletion effect in my numerous failed quit attempts. I have resisted the temptation to smoke for extended periods ranging from a few hours and sometimes for days but ultimately gave up. Just like in Baumeister's experimental condition, if I was engaged in another task that required willpower (for example, depriving myself of all distractions to focus and finish my report on time), I had no willpower left at the end of the day to resist smoking and would chain-smoke at least half a pack. I am convinced—by the scientific evidence and from my experience as a smoker—that willpower is a limited and consumable mental resource. At the same time, I also equivocally believe that one cannot quit smoking without the use of willpower.

It is not that you will have to resist the urge to smoke all day after quitting, but willpower must be at your disposal at all times. Typically, an urge to smoke only arises when somebody offers you a cigarette, or you find yourself in a situation where smoking used to be the default. In such instances, willpower is what you will be relying on to say no to smoking another cigarette.

Like everything else in life, you will have to learn to work with what you have. First, we will have to clear up some misconceptions about willpower. The gravest fallacy about willpower, by far, is the assumption that the *limited* nature of willpower means we have very little of it. We typically measure willpower as the length of time spent in deliberately pursuing a goal or restraining from an impulsive action. One can spend a few minutes, hours, weeks, months, or years pursuing a goal or resisting impulses. Your willpower can serve you for a few minutes for tasks such as reading a boring book, and yet you can persevere for years at other tasks such as following an investment plan so that you can retire with a million bucks. If all tasks consume and deplete a single pile of willpower, then why does our willpower last for different lengths of time, depending on the task at hand?

The limited nature of willpower is best understood analogically with money. I can quickly run out of both willpower and money, but the duration required to deplete these limited resources entirely depends on how much I have of it to start with. I can go broke in a month if I start with $1,000, but it will take considerably longer before I run out of a million dollars.

Great, but how do we know the amount of willpower we have at our beck and call for any given task? Researchers have shown that the amount of willpower at your disposal depends on how much you think you have of it in the first place. If you think that your capacity for self-control is limited and low, well, then you have low willpower [133, 155]. But if you think that your capacity to exert self-control is high or even unlimited, then you have a lot of it [133, 155]. It's all in your head! It is for this reason that one can persevere for years to become a top athlete, a musician, or an actor. We subconsciously believe that we have enough willpower for instances where we *must* or *want* to persevere. But our willpower will last only a few seconds at best when we find a delicious looking chocolate cake on the dining table. The same bag of willpower serves you differently depending on how you think of it.

Ergo, if you think that you have low willpower or are engaged in other tasks that demand willpower, you will have very little willpower left to say no when somebody offers you a cigarette. In situations that cause mental fatigue, your willpower will not take you very far in achieving your aspirations of someday becoming a nonsmoker

So, if you think you have very low willpower, here are your options. You can experiment using willpower in other aspects of your life, such as diet control or a strict bedtime routine. This will give you a more accurate assessment of your willpower and the extent to which you can push it. Over time you will develop more confidence to use your willpower. You can also prevent anything other than smoking from drawing on your limited reserve of willpower so that you can use it in a vulnerable situation. I suggest that you take both options, and I will show you how over the next few pages.

There is also a third option. Say that you can cover all your monthly expenses with $1,000. But in desperate situations, you can make the $1,000 last for more than a month with careful planning of your expenses. Similarly, you can stretch the duration required to deplete your willpower with a proper implementation plan, which is essentially an *if-this-happens-then-I-will-do-that* plan. A few years after the publication of Baumeister's study, researchers from the University of Sheffield showed that having an implementation plan increases persistence [156].

Most smokers who try to quit do so without thinking about how they will handle the urge to smoke in situations that they strongly associate with smoking. In most of my prior failed quit attempts, I did not create any plans to deal with high-pressure situations at work or major smoking cues such as going out for a few beers with my friends. When I encountered these situations, my effort to maintain the smoke-free status was running purely on willpower, which didn't last very long without an implementation plan.

I had learned from these mistakes and made simple plans to deal with all major and minor smoking triggers during my final quit attempt. I knew that the urge to smoke is strongest soon after waking up in the morning. I decided to buy an e-book reader and spend some time every morning reading a chapter or two from a book. Why an e-book reader, you might ask? Because unlike the rest of my family, I am an early riser, and reading physical books with the lights on is not an option. Also, I wanted to avoid getting out of bed immediately after waking up, as this would trigger my early morning smoking habit loop. The e-book reader solved these problems, and at the same time, I was engaging in a productive task to start my day. I was able to fight off the urge to smoke with a rewarding experience of reading an exciting book.

I created another simple plan to deal with the urge to smoke during social occasions, especially the ones involving alcohol. Going out with friends or colleagues in Japan usually means dinner and drinks. Conference dinners or academic networking events that I attend typically serve alcohol. And I don't have to try very hard to convince a smoker that the urge to smoke is strong with alcohol. Here is my plan to deal with such situations: if I knew beforehand that I would be tired or stressed on the day of an event, I either reorganized the day to make it lighter or politely refused to attend. If I had accepted the invitation but felt tired on the day, then I made a last-minute cancellation. If I could not avoid attending, I would alternate my drinks with a glass of water instead of cigarettes.

Another vulnerable social context is when you catch up with your smoking buddies at work. For a couple of weeks after I quit smoking, I brought along an *Umeboshi Onigiri* (rice balls with Japanese salt plums), a banana, or an orange (occasionally orange juice) instead of my usual coffee and cigarettes to a meeting with my smoking buddies. Fortunately, these situations are not as tricky as the ones with alcohol, and I was able to meet my smoking buddies without the slightest urge to smoke in about two weeks, after which I no longer needed an implementation plan. My implementation plan with alcohol lasted well over a year.

A particularly useful implementation plan that I created was to deal with an intense urge to smoke before a lecture or a research presentation. I learned to use cigarettes to deal with my stage fright in the early years of college life. But by the time I was through with my doctoral research, I had substantial practice with lecturing and conference presentations and was no longer afraid of standing in front of an audience. But the habit of smoking before facing an audience had stuck. During my final quit attempt, I planned to deal with such situations by strolling just before the lecture. I mentally rehearsed the contents of my talk during these casual walks, most of which lasted less than ten minutes.

Some of these *if-this-happens-then-I-will-do-that* plans were useful for a few weeks and when no longer necessary automatically weaned out. For example, just a few weeks after I quit smoking, I no longer needed to take a banana or an orange to intellectually charged discussion with a smoker friend. Other *if-this-happens-then-I-will-do-that* plans have developed into a strong habit over time. For example, now I habitually alternate water and alcoholic drinks and go for a short walk before a lecture.

These experiences, though simple, were impactful. Each strategy was rewarding, and I learned that passing on the opportunities to smoke further strengthened my resolve to quit smoking. My brain perceived the execution of these implementation plans as a victory and rewarded me by providing a neurochemical high. Over time these small victories add up by building confidence and resolve to escape from the cycle of quitting and relapse permanently.

Perhaps you were already aware of the facts I have presented thus far about willpower: that it is a limited resource and the amount of willpower you have depends on how much you believe you have of it. But what you may not know is that it is possible to increase the amount of willpower you have. In this regard, willpower is like a muscle—the more you exercise, the stronger your muscle gets.

Some experts liken willpower to a muscle that can get fatigued from overuse [157]. But if you deliberately overuse your muscles to grow them, you will be looking at a bulked up, Arnold Schwarzenegger-like physique after several months of an intense workout. Indeed, numerous studies on ego depletion effect show that persistence increases with deliberate practice [158-161]. Practicing small acts of self-control before quitting smoking reduces your chance of relapse [159]. This is one of the reasons why I asked you to track your daily smoking expenses using a smartphone app in the previous chapter. Habit tracking requires persistence and self-control, and this can serve as a practice for using willpower.

The analogy between willpower and muscle does not end there. Willpower requires energy in the form of glucose, just like your muscle depends on glucose for energy. Even simple acts of self-control lower your blood glucose below normal levels, and exerting more willpower becomes impossible [162]. Consequently, using willpower drains your body of energy. As a natural response to low blood glucose, your body craves more calories, and we know that the hunger pangs caused by low blood glucose ultimately leads to obesity [163]. So, if you are frequently relying on willpower to quit smoking, your body will also crave for food more often. Therefore, people put on the extra pounds when they quit on crude willpower. Don't be alarmed; I will discuss ways to deal with post-quitting weight gain in the penultimate chapter on *Maintenance.*

I hope you will use these crucial findings from willpower research as you approach your quit date. Practice using willpower for small acts such as relinquishing the morning coffee for a couple of days; on other days, avoid the donut or the pretzel that you usually snack on. Stop using mints and gums altogether or track your smoking-related expense using a smartphone app for a couple of weeks. These activities will help train your willpower muscle.

Also, adjust your meal times to coincide with your usual smoking times of the day to ensure that your body has a sufficient supply of glucose to fuel willpower. If not all meals, you can at least adjust your breakfast time. I used to skip my breakfast on most days as a smoker because of which I was smoking more during the mornings than in the afternoons or the evenings. Most smokers I know either entirely skip breakfast or eat poorly in the morning, making the morning cigarette the hardest to resist. Your body awakens hungry and dehydrated after six to eight hours of sleep. Naturally, your blood glucose is lowest when you wake up, and so is your ability to use willpower. Start your day with a banana, half a glass of orange juice, or a slice of bread with peanut butter to boost your morning blood glucose levels in the run-up to your quit day. These foods are quickly absorbed and rapidly increase your blood sugar level. My preference was orange juice, as this is quick-acting (provides both sugar and hydration) and requires no preparation at all. In any case, avoid starting with coffee or tea. Several studies have confirmed that caffeine increases the urge to smoke [164, 165].

In sum, you should practice using willpower for small acts in the week preceding your quit date so that you increase your reserve of willpower before you take the plunge. You should also modify the timings of your meals to ensure you are not running on low blood sugar. If you feel that you lack strong willpower, then you might want to eliminate other habits or tasks that require using willpower, especially for two or three weeks after your quit date. You want to save most, if not all, of your willpower for resisting the urge to smoke. The next section will help you do that.

Isolate the cigarette

If you have been reading this book for a few days and have followed my three original instructions, you should be used to smoking mindfully by now. Once you isolate your cigarette, you will start to notice the power of this advice. When smoking is the only activity you are engaged in and are fully aware of your sensations, emotions, and thoughts, you will realize the bitter taste of smoke, the irritation in your throat and lungs, and the increased pulse around your temple and wrists. As you suck on one end of the cigarette, ask yourself if the smoke is relaxing you. Visualize the blood carrying seven thousand toxic chemicals to your brain and how they harm your ability to think critically and creatively. No, this is not meditation; it is mindful smoking, but the experience is equally surreal. Researchers from Yale University have demonstrated that mindfulness training [fn16] helps smokers cut down the number of cigarettes smoked per day and also makes the process of quitting easier [166]. I am sure that no rational human being is capable of smoking cigarettes while being fully aware of the experience it creates.

For most smokers, isolating the cigarette is easier said than done. The habit of smoking is a complex one, and lighting up the cigarette is only a part of it. The other things you do while smoking, such as drinking coffee or flipping through your smartphone, also becomes part of the larger habit. Therefore, smoking is not one habit; it is a collection of smaller habits. Authors Charles Duhigg ("The Power of Habit"), James Clear ("Atomic Habits"), S.J. Scott ("Habit Stacking"), B.J. Fogg ("Tiny Habits"), and others have called this process habit stacking.

My smoking habit incorporated several new habits over time and became a massive stack of different habits. In the first few months, the morning cigarette was not a necessity. As the habit of smoking grew stronger, the duration between waking up in the morning and my first cigarette of the day shortened. Soon, I needed a cigarette first thing after

---

[fn16] This training taught the study participants to observe how cravings feel in the body and how thoughts, emotions, and body sensations become triggers for craving and smoking. The participants were also introduced to a technique to 'mindfully' work with cravings (Recognize, Accept, Investigate, and Note what cravings feel like as they arise, acronym: RAIN).

waking up. This created the need to add coffee to my first-thing-in-the-morning-cigarette ritual to deal with the dry throat caused by dehydration after eight hours of sleep. Ultimately, my morning smoking ritual became a collection of habits that included getting out of bed, walk to the kitchen, prepare instant coffee, walk to the balcony, light up a cigarette, and then go to the bathroom. This was my pre-marriage habit stack for the first cigarette of the day. After marriage, I smoked my first cigarette only after I left the house for work to avoid exposing my wife to secondhand smoke. I quickly created a new habit stack—bike to the nearest coffee shop, buy a coffee, smoke my first cigarette, and then head to work.

If I skipped this habit stack for whatever reason, the first cigarette wouldn't be as satisfying, and I usually smoked two back-to-back cigarettes. Without coffee, even the back-to-back cigarettes did not adequately relieve the craving. I was addicted to this stack as a whole.

If you ritualize any of your cigarettes, as most smokers do, then you need to isolate the cigarette from the other components of the ritual. Most smokers tend to ritualize the morning cigarette, the first cigarette after getting to work, or the after-meal cigarette. Unstack the habit and isolate the cigarette before you set the quit date.

Unstack your smoking habit is an essential step. You have become habituated to each component of the habit stack. When you quit smoking, the chances are that you will also be entirely or partially eliminating the non-cigarette parts of your habit stack. You need to deal with these non-cigarette parts of your habit stack first so that they do not use up your willpower when you quit smoking (and this can be great practice to extend your willpower reserves). I was addicted to coffee, but only when it was part of my smoking habit stack. I enjoyed my cigarettes better with coffee. Parting with the coffee was as hard as letting go of the ritualized cigarette itself. When I finally kicked the habit of smoking, I had already eliminated coffee as a part of ritualized smoking, and my limited resource of willpower was fully available for fending off the urge to smoke another cigarette.

The three most important things to isolated the cigarette from are: smoking accessories (especially products such as coffee, mints, or gums), the place where you usually smoke, and the time when you regularly smoke. You will be able to unstack your habit completely in a couple of weeks. In the first week, dissociate the easiest part of the habit stack, which is the use of other products that support your smoking behavior. For example, smoke your cigarette and then make coffee (if you cannot do without coffee) or vice versa. But in any case, do not drink coffee while smoking your cigarette. Stop buying mints altogether. The idea is to do just one thing at a time.

When you are no longer dependent on other products to support the smoking habit, work to isolate the cigarette from places where you usually smoke. You associate the usual place of smoking with peace, joy, or a brief escape from drudgery and is therefore slightly more difficult than getting rid of coffees, mints, and gums. Avoid your usual smoking area and rotate your smoking breaks in other smoking areas near you. If this causes inconvenience, then that's a bonus. The more inconvenient smoking becomes, the easier it will be to end the relationship.

You will be taking things to a whole new level when you start to isolate the cigarette from the times of the day when you regularly smoke. You will essentially be practicing quitting smoking but for short periods. You only need to break up the morning cigarette, and the rest will take care of itself. The easiest way to disrupt your smoking pattern is to delay the first cigarette of the day by one hour compared to the previous day. If you smoked your first cigarette at 6 am yesterday, then delay the first cigarette to 7 am today. Spend the extra one hour working from home, catching up on pending tasks, cleaning your room, preparing a healthy breakfast, or reading a book. Delay by an additional hour on all subsequent days. If you fail to keep the target on a particular day, do not give up or restart; pick up from where you left off. If it helps, print a calendar for the current month (easily and freely downloadable on the internet) and note the time of the first cigarette of the day. (I have provided an example on the following page.) Physical proof of your progress will go a long way in strengthening your motivation and expanding your willpower.

As you continue to delay the first cigarette by an hour each day, you will start to feel the itch that something is not right or is incomplete. This itch is a sign that your brain is craving a ritualized habit. Don't resist—give it one that is not associated with cigarettes. This is the perfect time for you to create and implement your counter-conditioning strategy, which is essentially a new ritualized habit that will supersede the smoking habit.

Sun	Mon	Tue	Wed	Thu	Fri	Sat
		1 Smoked @ 6 am	2 Smoked @ 7 am	3 Smoked @ 6 am	4 Smoked @ 8 am	5 Smoked @ 9 am
6 Smoked @ 10 am	7 Smoked @ 11 am	8 Smoked @ 12 am	9 Smoked @ 1 pm	10 Smoked @ 2 pm	11 Quit day	12 Smoke-free
13 Smoke-free	14 Smoke-free	15 Smoke-free	16 Smoke-free	17 Smoke-free	18 Smoke-free	19 Smoke-free
20 Smoke-free	21 Smoke-free	22 Smoke-free	23 Smoke-free	24 Smoke-free	25 Smoke-free	26 Smoke-free
27 Smoke-free	28 Smoke-free	29 Smoke-free	30 Smoke-free	31 Smoke-free		

Create a counter-conditioning plan

There will be numerous instances during the process of quitting smoking when it will be necessary for you to use willpower. What will you do if you meet a smoker friend over drinks later this week, and given the familiar environment and company, an irresistible urge to smoke kicks in? Play Candy Crush? Pretend to smoke your ridiculous mock cigarette rolled out of heavy paper? Ignore your friend and listen to music? You would rather smoke than participate in any of these socially awkward behaviors. This is where willpower is incredibly useful. Willpower is like a universally accepted credit card, albeit with a credit limit. It is always available for use. And the best part is that it is invisible, weightless, free, replenishable, does not occupy any space in your bag or wallet, and you don't have to be worried about forgetting it on the kitchen table.

It is, therefore, important that you maximize your reserve of willpower and ensure that it is full before you quit smoking. As discussed before, practicing the use of willpower, creating a strong motivation to quit, and creating a well-crafted counter-conditioning and stimulus control plan all increase your reserve of willpower. Addressing other unnecessary tasks and habits that requires willpower before you quit will also ensure that it is exclusively available to combat the urge to smoke if and when it hits.

Although willpower is vital to help you quit smoking, it is a limited resource and will not be enough to maintain your new-found status of being a nonsmoker forever. It is too much of a risk to solely rely on willpower to quit. As they say, don't put all your eggs in one basket. Save your willpower for emergencies and let the counter-conditioning and stimulus control strategies do most of the heavy lifting.

Counter-conditioning and stimulus control are fundamentally different and deserve separate discussions as one replaces the act of smoking, and the other helps you deal with smoking triggers. Let's tackle counter-conditioning first and understand the features of an effective counter-conditioning strategy.

As I have emphasized several times in earlier chapters, you will be re-experiencing almost everything as a nonsmoker. While most of the re-experiencing is fun, some can be quite confusing. Ironically, it is the positive gains of quitting that is most confusing. You will have so much energy and time after you quit that you will not know what to do with it. Too much energy and free time is a recipe for impulsivity and can fuel other bad habits. I have seen people go on shopping, eating, and Netflix-watching spree after quitting, not knowing how to deal with the extra time and energy. The immediately observable results of these unproductive acts, such as increasing credit card debt and waistline, will negate all the hard work we put into becoming a nonsmoker. It is only natural to think of these negative effects as a consequence of quitting smoking. Relapse then becomes inevitable. If you are determined to quit, you must anticipate such issues and create a good counter-conditioning technique that prevents you from spiraling into yet another cycle of quitting and relapse. This gives us the first criterion for what constitutes a good counter-conditioning strategy: *Counter-conditioning strategies must not produce any negative effects.*

Naturally, the counter-conditioning strategy must have positive effects. But that is as ambiguous as a statement can be. Fortunately, we have already laid the ground-work for the precise positive effects expected from a counter-conditioning strategy in the previous chapter on *Determination*. The positive gains in money, health, and time—the three big motivators to quit smoking—are not immediately obvious after quitting. *A good counter-conditioning strategy must make the gains in money, health, and time (or any other motivation that you may have) immediately observable.* As you will soon see, this is much easier to do than it sounds.

To understand the third criterion for a good counter-conditioning strategy, we need to revisit the process of habit formation briefly. As discussed earlier, you create new habits when you repeat the same action in response to a cue. To ensure that the habit is automatically performed, the brain rewards you with a neurochemical high by releasing dopamine that activates the reward circuits in the brain. Once a habit is firmly established with an emotional appeal, it becomes an automatic response. If you experience a familiar cue, then you will instinctively perform a set action. In the first few weeks as a nonsmoker, I instinctively reached for the pack in my pockets after buying my morning coffee only to realize that I am not a smoker anymore. My habit loop of morning coffee (cue)-need a cigarette (craving)-light up a cigarette (action)-neurochemical high of dopamine (reward) had fired up automatically. My response to this particular habit loop: shrugged my shoulder with an evil smile on my face as I walked out. I may have even managed to freak out the lady entering the coffee shop.

I know from the testimonies of hundreds of smokers that many have tried to modify the habit loop as a way to break the smoking habit. For example, some have tried to replace the action (smoking) to a familiar cue (e.g., stressful situations) with chocolates, snacks, vaping, and music. This idea to substitute one activity with another has gained popularity after several bestselling books on habit. But the repetition of a specific set of cue-craving-action-reward is how habits are formed, and replacing the action does not break the habit. Replacing smoking with snacking creates a new habit. Your new habit (stressful event-craving for stress relief-SNACKING-neurochemical high) will only supersede the old habit (stressful event-craving for stress relief-LIGHT UP A CIGARETTE-neurochemical high) if it is emotionally more appealing. If it is not, you will be heavily relying on willpower to quit smoking.

As discussed in part one, smoking is an incredibly emotional experience because of the multitude of influences and reasons that led us into the trap of smoking the first cigarette. Most smokers, especially those who started at an early age, did not learn to deal with their emotional problems with candies, gums, chocolates, potato chips, finger fidgets, or squeeze balls. Even if you did, these products did not have the same emotional appeal as a cigarette. Consequently, no consumer product can have a greater emotional appeal than a cigarette. Moreover, most consumer products, such as food, candies, and chocolates, violate the first criterion by increasing your body weight. We now have the third criterion for a good counter conditioning plan. *Do not use another consumer product to replace the habit of smoking.* Since you are not addicted to nicotine, you also won't be needing nicotine patches, gums, e-cigarettes, and inhalers.

The final criterion for a good counter-conditioning technique that we have covered many times in earlier sections is sustainability. Current evidence indicates that successful quitters rely on counter-conditioning techniques for at least twenty-four months [167]. On the other hand, relapsers use counter-conditioning techniques for only about twelve months and then give up [167]. Your counter-conditioning plan must, therefore, be relatively easy and inexpensive to sustain for at least two years. Below is the summary list of the criteria for creating an effective counter-conditioning plan:

- Must not produce any negative effects such as weight gain.

- Must make the gains in the primary motivators (money, health, and time) after quitting immediately observable.

- Must have a greater emotional appeal than cigarettes. This criterion excludes most consumer products.

- Must be easy to do, inexpensive, and sustainable for at least two years.

I fully realize that this is a strict set of criteria—too tight some might say—but a strong adversary requires an equally strong response. I know of three things that satisfy all these criteria, and I continue to use all of them to this day. You are more than welcome to try these or experiment with others, but remember that it is essential that any counter-conditioning strategy you use satisfies the four-point criteria.

The first counter-conditioning strategy that I used was food tracking with the help of a popular smartphone-based app [fn17]. The goal was to develop healthier eating habits, lose the excess weight I had gained over the years, and prevent post-quitting weight gain. Remember Peter Drucker's words of wisdom: "What gets measured, gets managed." Food diary helped in many ways. It helped me eat my calories in four moderately sized meals instead of two huge meals. I used to skip some meals as a smoker, usually breakfast. As a result, I was eating two meals a day of roughly a thousand calories each and a snack of about four hundred calories. After quitting, and as a direct result of diet tracking, I eat three meals a day of about six hundred calories each, and my snack is usually a

---

[fn17] I prefer MyFitnessPal for food tracking because of their massive database of food. I know that there are other apps out there but have not tried any of them.

fruit and yogurt that adds two hundred calories to my daily intake. Diet tracking also helped me see, for the very first time, just how many calories smoking was indirectly adding to my daily diet. A cup of coffee and a can of soda to go with my morning and after work cigarettes added another three hundred calories. I was consuming nearly three thousand calories a day as a smoker with two large meals and slightly over two thousand calories spread out across three meals as a nonsmoker.

This is what makes willpower very interesting—one can look at it as a limited resource or as a self-sustaining resource. Earlier, I presented scientific evidence to show that deliberate practice increases persistence. Before quitting, I practiced self-control and perseverance by tracking my diet, among other things. Then I quit smoking, and it is an understatement to say that this was a major test for self-control and persistence. This meant more practice with willpower. With so much practice, I was able to resist certain foods and maintain a healthy and well-balanced diet after quitting without much trouble.

I paid particular attention to water intake as a part of my balanced diet post-quitting. Water is an often ignored nutrient but is, in fact, the most important part of a healthy diet. Both hydration and a healthy diet are essential after quitting. Earlier I discussed how glucose is indispensable to maintaining willpower, and water is required by your body to repair itself after you quit smoking. Moreover, hydration is important to decrease impulsivity as well as food cravings. I will discuss food, water, and weight gain after quitting in the chapter on *Maintenance*.

The second counter-conditioning plan that I implemented was running. I aimed to run five kilometers four times a week in the mornings. This is by far, my favorite strategy because this takes time (almost an hour during the first month to run 5K), energy, and the results are immediately visible. I tracked my runs using an app that piggybacked on my smartphone's GPS to give accurate data on the distance covered and pace [fn18]. I could see the dramatic improvements in my fitness every week. My pace went from

---

[fn18] I have tried virtually all apps that can track your workout and finally settled for Strava. It is simple, easy to use, has a social element to it (like Facebook, but for runners), and connects well with my other fitness apps. I later connected a Wahoo chest strap heart rate monitor to Strava to get additional data.

eleven minutes to six minutes for every kilometer in the first thirty days. I was able to shave off another minute over the next two months. Not only was I running faster, but I was also running longer distances. After three months of quitting smoking, I was running ten kilometers five times a week. This required extra focus on my diet and hydration, and the first counter-conditioning plan to track my diet paid off here. At the end of six months of quitting, I had lost fourteen kilograms (nearly 31 lbs.) and had run my first twenty-kilometer race. I topped that in the following month by running my first marathon at the age of thirty-one. Running was a natural way to exploit my new-found fitness but also to accelerate the recovery from years of damage caused by smoking.

You don't necessarily have to run a marathon for staying quit. Moderate levels of physical exercise can also increase willpower with additional perks, such as decreased perceived stress and better emotional control [168]. Moderate exercise also lowers the consumption of cigarettes, alcohol, and caffeine and promotes healthy eating [168]. Walking, the simplest forms of physical activity, or weekend hiking produce similar positive effects.

I admit that I am heavily biased towards running and walking, and this is not without reason. The results of these simple exercises are immediately visible, even without smartphone-based tracking. You will notice improvements in your breathing, stamina, and overall mood in just a couple of days. Moreover, these activities are inexpensive, do not require any specialized gear other than a good pair of shoes, and you can do them almost anywhere (important if you are a globetrotter).

But the last counter-conditioning plan probably had the most substantial positive impact on my life. I had for years heard about financial independence but had never aspired towards achieving this goal [fn19]. I began tracking my smoking-related expense about three months before I quit smoking, and in just the first month, I realized that the habit was

---

[fn19] If financial independence is of interest to you then I suggest the following titles. They are excellent resources on the topic and written by people with specialized knowledge.
- *The Total Money Makeover* by Dave Ramsey (Thomas Nelson Inc)
- *The Millionaire Fastlane* by MJ DeMarco (Viperion Publishing Corp)
- *The Compound Effect* by Darren Hardy (Vanguard Press)
- *Rich Dad Poor Dad* by Robert T. Kiyosaki (Plata Publishing)

gobbling at least a fifth of my income. If I added this amount to the 15 percent that I was already saving, I could be financially independent in a decade. My calculations were off by the distance to the moon and back. As of this writing, I expect to be financially independent in the next eighteen months—nearly six years before I thought I could. This means that I will not have to depend on my salary for income. I will be free to do whatever I want to do with my time: travel, write more books, become a full-time father, or continue research and teaching at the university. This alone is a strong motivator to not waste another dime on an unproductive and useless habit like smoking.

In case you are thinking that quitting destroyed my math skills, let me assure you that this is not the case. Underestimating my saving potential was also an effect of quitting smoking. I had not factored the unbelievable change in my productivity post-quitting. I was offered a new position within the university soon after quitting, which came with a raise. The extra time spent reading books expanded my thinking. I had more ideas and more time to execute the ideas. The daily runs helped me think clearly and develop those ideas even further. Some of the ideas became books, like the one you are holding right now, and others became academic skills development seminars.

Diet, exercise, and financial planning are the crown jewels of my counter-conditioning strategy because they are keystones habits that have a positive impact on multiple aspects of your life. A few other strategies, however, deserve honorable re-mentions. Reading is a great way to relax and yet engage in a productive task. E-readers have made it easier to take all your favorite books everywhere you go. Moreover, e-readers are discreet, and you can read whatever you like without the fear of people judging your choices. If you prefer listening, you can now purchase the audiobook version of popular books. In earlier chapters, I discussed going for a brief walk before a lecture, alternating drinks with water, and a healthy snack instead of the usual coffee and cigarettes when catching up with smoking buddies, at least for the first two weeks as a nonsmoker.

Although these honorable mentions are not very emotional acts, and they do not make the gains of quitting smoking obvious, they served as useful counter-conditioning techniques by replacing the act of smoking in highly vulnerable situations. My three crown jewels are as useless as Candy Crush if I am meeting a smoker friend over lunch and the urges to smoke returns as he lights his after-lunch cigarette. It is, therefore, important to have an overarching counter-conditioning strategy such as achieving physical or financial fitness as well as context-specific strategies such as drinking a glass of water between Jack Daniels. Ideally, the context-specific strategy must not be dramatic and overtly visible to others like finger fidgets or squeeze balls, which are difficult to sustain over long periods. Your plan should blend in subtlety as if part of your everyday life. Doing something natural such as drinking water between beers, reading, or strolling, is more sustainable because these are rewarding experiences on their own. Imagine waking up after a night out with friends fully fresh and with no hangover. Even small positive experiences can be a gratifying experience for the brain and will help to reinforce the idea that you are making significant strides towards becoming a permanent nonsmoker.

Stimulus control

Stimulus control techniques, by definition, should help you avoid or deal with situations that trigger the urge to smoke. However, we need to look at the issue of avoiding and dealing with triggers separately as one of them will lead you into relapse.

Current evidence indicates that successful quitters increasingly rely on stimulus control techniques for at least the first twelve months and maintain the same level of dependency over the second year of quitting [167]. On the other hand, relapsers use stimulus control techniques similar to successful quitters for only about eighteen months, after which their use of stimulus control is almost non-existent [167]. Evidently, having a stimulus control plan, at least for the first eighteen months, does not predict your chances of permanently quitting smoking. We have aggregated so many cues to smoking over time that it will be impossible to avoid things, places, or situations forever without excessively relying on willpower. Therefore, stimulus control that involves avoiding a smoking trigger has limited utility in helping you stay smoke-free.

During my last failed quit attempt, I quit smoking for about three months. It was effortless. I had no cravings or any major withdrawal symptoms. I had no urge to smoke whatsoever, even in the company of other smokers. But then I met Sid, a close friend that I had been avoiding for quite some time (stimulus control!). Sid and I have spent countless hours debating scientific issues, politics, religion, and the validity of the flat earth theory (sorry flat-earthers, no love from me.) Of course, we enjoyed these debates with a coffee and a few cigarettes. When I eventually met him, smoking was completely off my mind. As always, we were discussing an intellectually demanding topic when I suddenly felt a strong urge to smoke. Sid was already into his second cigarette by then. The situation was overly familiar and demanded a cigarette. I resisted for a few minutes and then gave in to the offer to smoke. I met Sid several times over the next few weeks, and the same pattern repeated. I was firm about not smoking before the meetings, resisted for a few minutes during, and then smoked a cigarette (or two). I had wholly relapsed at the end of three weeks and was back on my pack-a-day routine.

I have spent hours dissecting this event. Why did I give in to smoking after staying quit for three months? Why could I resist smoking when in the company of other smokers but caved in the company of a close friend? I still don't have a clear answer to why I relapsed the way I did, but I had learned a fundamental lesson through this failed quit attempt—*do not avoid situations where smoking was your default action in the past.*

You must learn to deal with any situation you can imagine as a trigger. You will inevitably come across smokers and situations that remind you of smoking unless the politicians have a sudden change in heart and ban smoking altogether. Step one is to break down your smoking triggers and identify those that need special attention. Three types of triggers have the potential to remind you of smoking: *irrelevant*, *avoidable*, and *workable stimuli*. The first two are not strong enough to cause relapse, but the workable stimulus is, hence, the name.

After you quit smoking, you will no longer need to visit certain places. For example, I no longer needed to visit the designated smoking area outside the university campus after I quit smoking. Consequently, these places became irrelevant as a cue to smoking. The same also applied to my portable ashtray and lighter. I got rid of these smoking accessories on my quit day, and they were irrelevant afterward.

I was also able to avoid certain situations as a nonsmoker. Before my quit day, I would almost always say yes to an invitation for drinks or dinner from my smoking buddies. After I quit, I was able to say no most of the time. I was more in control over when I was exposing myself to environments that would create a strong urge to smoke. Similarly, I also had control over when and where I drink coffee (a strong smoking cue for me). I was able to avoid drinking coffee in vulnerable situations and instead grabbed a bottle of water, hot chocolate, or a cuppa. These were my avoidable stimuli.

When we avoid these stimuli, most smokers feel, as I felt, that we are successfully suppressing, controlling, or avoiding our urges to smoke. Do not be carried away by the false sense of accomplishment. You don't have to put in extra effort to avoid irrelevant and avoidable stimuli, and they kick in automatically once you quit smoking. The real monster lurking under the water is a workable stimulus.

Triggers that can be categories as a workable stimulus are not obvious and are therefore difficult to spot. Most smokers are oblivious to the strength of the bonding they share with smoking in certain situations. Some relationships, experiences, and habits emerge purely because of smoking. I met Sid, and many other close friends, at designated smoking areas. All my intellectually charged discussions in academia have been over cigarettes. And all my milestone and achievements after the age of fifteen was marked by a *victory cigarette* and some alone time. Naturally, these situations have strong associations with smoking, but the power of these associations only became evident after I quit smoking.

In my last and final relapse, I had failed to address the impetus provided by the context of meeting a close friend and what I considered a quality discussion. I had not thought about what I would do in situations like these if the urge to smoke strikes. I even failed to consider the possibility that my resolve to quit smoking was vulnerable with a close friend that I strongly associated with smoking. I was not going to make the same mistake again.

As difficult as it may be to spot a workable stimulus, the solution is remarkably simple. During my subsequent (and successful) quit attempt, I made a list of all possible scenarios where I truly enjoyed smoking. This was a relatively short list and included a stimulating conversation, engaging in deep work, out drinking with friends, and rare moments of peace.

I was embarrassed when I created this list. I have had a great upbringing, a good education, a dream job, a fair share of professional success, and an unbelievably selfless and loving family. Why was I not at peace? My mind was so busy, all the time, that I had to mark the rare experience of peace with the pleasure of smoking a cigarette. Similarly, I questioned why the already rewarding experiences of a stimulating conversation, engaging in deep work, and spending time with friends was not enough that I had to add a cigarette (or a pack of cigarettes to be more accurate) to make these experiences special?

The simple answer is that I did not know how to experience these things without a cigarette. My faculties of critical thinking, working with deep focus, and even considering mental peace and tranquility as a real thing only developed in adulthood somewhere between the age of eighteen and twenty-two. By the age of eighteen, I had already been a smoker for three years, and all subsequent life experiences were as a smoker. I simply did not know how to enjoy my time with friends, engage in focused work, or appreciate rare moments of peace without a cigarette.

This revelation hit the reset button for me. The researcher in me was thrilled at the prospect of comparing the experience with and without smoking. This need to re-experience everything as a nonsmoker served as a self-sustaining source of motivation and made the process of quitting more enjoyable and purposeful. The trick was not to avoid situations that would trigger smoking, but instead, experience each situation first hand as a nonsmoker.

Any life experience that you experienced for the first time after you started smoking is potentially a workable stimulus. You should have already compiled a list of your workable stimulus in part one; if not, please revisit and complete Task#3 at the end of part one. While the prospect of re-experiencing situations as a nonsmoker for the first time is thrilling, a workable stimulus is probably the most prominent trigger to smoke. Smoking has always been your default state in these situations.

But, I promised that the solution to workable stimuli would be remarkably easy. Even better, the solution applies to any situation that can trigger an urge to smoke and is the only one-shoe-fits-all strategy in this book. The solution to workable stimuli came to me whole and complete—gift-wrapped, you could say—when I read the story of Michael Phelps (no, not his pot-smoking days) and his exploits at the Olympic games in *Psychology Today* (a semi-academic magazine). Phelps is the most decorated Olympian of all time with a total of twenty-eight medals. Phelps won eight gold medals in just one Olympic game (the 2008 Beijing Olympics). If he were a country, he would rank thirty-five on the all times Olympic medal table with more gold medals than 170 out of 206 countries competing in the games. How did Phelps achieve this incredible feat?

Both Phelps and his coach Bob Bowman attribute this success story to Phelps's ability to visualize the ideal swim right down to the intimate details. Each night Phelps mentally rehearsed the perfect swim before he went to bed, and in the morning, he would practice swimming with blinded goggles. This routine paid off during the final race of the 200m butterfly event in the Beijing Olympics. Phelps's goggles started to fill-up during the race, and he was essentially swimming blind. Phelps not only won the race; he broke the world record. Because of his quirky visualization routine, Phelps was able to quickly adapt when disaster struck. The mental practice had prepared him for all worst-case scenarios and how to deal with them.

Several athletes and chess masters have used visualization to rehearse their actions mentally in preparation for the big event. Tiger Woods and Muhammad Ali have both used visualization for achieving sporting success in their respective fields. But my favorite example—one that is fit for a movie script—is that of Natan Sharansky, who was incarcerated by the former USSR for nine years on charges of spying. Sharansky, who was also a chess prodigy, used his time in confinement, visualizing the perfect game of chess. In 1996, Sharansky beat Garry Kasparov, the greatest of the greats.

Please do not confuse the process of visualization with imagination. Visualization is far more detailed and includes recreating a mental experience of sound, sight, smell, taste, and touch. When I read Phelps' story and how he used visualization, it sounded like magic to me. It was much like the book *The Secret* and its central premise, the Law of Attraction (which is incidentally one of the few books I couldn't read to the end). My scientific training has programmed me—for good or bad—to seek evidence for anything that sounds implausible, and visualization certainly fits the bill. Imagining an action, or even better an outcome, into reality was tantamount to extraterrestrials building the pyramids. How could a thought manifest into physical reality?

Luckily, I didn't throw out the idea of visualization. I don't know if it was because I was desperately seeking for a stimulus control technique or due to my awareness of numerous instances of the power of mind over body in medicine—placebo and nocebo effects being the most common—I decided to look up more information on the subject. It took less than an hour for me to realize that the skepticism on this issue was due to my ignorance of the subject. There was evidence, better yet from well-controlled scientific studies, for the effectiveness of visualization. Numerous studies have shown that the brain reacts to imagined muscle contraction as if it is real exercise and produces significant increases in muscle strength [169-171]. Visualization also enables people to develop original and practical inventions and to make creative artistic drawings [172]. Mental practice is even being used clinically to restore the function of limbs, daily activity, and skills of patients paralyzed by stroke [173-176].

Determined to be the Michael Phelps of quitting smoking, I imagined the events of the following day that were likely to trigger the urge to smoke. I performed this routine every day at bedtime for about a week before quitting and three weeks after. I envisioned meeting my smoker friends, working in deep focus, and celebrating with friends in granular detail. I tried to imagine the smell of stale smoke, the dirty ashtrays, and the irritation caused by cigarette smoke to my eyes. I then imagined an intense urge to smoke, which often manifested physically. But because I was already in bed and sleepy, I rarely got up to light a cigarette. I also rehearsed thinking about why I was smoking and what smoking was doing for me while smoking an imaginary cigarette. On most nights, I fell asleep while carrying out the visualization routine. Surprisingly, the more I did this bedtime ritual, my disgust for cigarettes grew stronger in the morning.

The power of this visualization ritual became apparent when I encountered familiar situations that would otherwise trigger the urge to smoke. In most cases, the situations no longer created an urge to smoke; and when it did, I was able to fight off these urges with willpower. Envisioning a vulnerable situation in advance somehow made me more resilient in real life. Perhaps the mental practice had expanded my bag of willpower or made my willpower muscle stronger. After three years, visualization has become one of my keystone habits, like exercise, with a positive impact on several aspects of my life.

In any case, visualization is so effective as a stimulus control technique that I didn't need another one. The only other strategy that I have tried and can be a stimulus control technique of sorts was deep breathing. I consider deep breathing only a part stimulus control technique because I used it primarily to correct my breathing. Smokers tend to develop a characteristic shallow breathing pattern [fn20], which is barely noticeable in everyday life but becomes obvious during exercise. I programmed myself to think of urges and cravings as a reminder to restore my normal breathing pattern. Also, taking deep breaths is relaxing and helps clear up your mind.

You can use visualization or deep breathing as your stimulus control technique or create one of your own. Irrespective of the technique, remember that an effective stimulus control technique has two things in common with good counter-conditioning strategy: they must not produce any negative effects such as weight gain and must be easy to do, inexpensive, and sustainable for at least two years.

[fn20] Not to be confused with shortness of breath. In shallow breathing, the duration of inhaling and exhaling is shorter than normal breathing but have equal cadence. Comparatively, inhalation is much shorter than exhalation in shortness of breath.

Chapter Summary

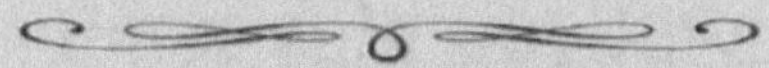

✓ Willpower is a limited but powerful resource. The use of willpower can be extended by good nutrition, small acts of self-control, and by having an implementation plan.

✓ Conserve your willpower by unstacking the habit and isolating the cigarette. Besides, this will help in mindful smoking.

✓ Replacing the action in a habit loop (cue-craving-action-reward) creates a new habit.

✓ Only when the new habit is emotionally more appealing, it will supersede the old one.

✓ A good counter-conditioning technique should not produce adverse effects and must make the gains of quitting obvious, have a greater emotional appeal than cigarettes, and be sustainable for at least two years.

✓ Improving one's diet, engaging in physical activity, and financial planning are great counter-conditioning strategies.

✓ Create stimulus control techniques to deal with your urges. The best stimulus control technique is visualization. Envisioning yourself in a vulnerable situation makes you more resilient.

✓ Realizing that everything is a brand-new experience as a nonsmoker will help you enjoy the process of quitting.

Task #6
How will you stay smoke-free after quitting?

Counter-conditioning strategies (Activities to replace smoking)

1. ____

2. ____

3. ____

4. ____

5. ____

Stimulus control strategies (Plans to deal with triggers, urges, and cravings)

1. ____

2. ____

3. ____

4. ____

5. ____

Action: Establish the when and how of quitting

Vision without action is merely a dream. Action without vision just passes the time. Vision with action can change the world.

-Joel A. Barker, author and futurist

There are two concerns around the act of quitting, both simple. The first one is about the timing of smoking the last cigarette and the second around the method to quit—abruptly or gradually. I will address both concerns in this chapter.

I know, from my interaction with current smokers who are trying to quit smoking, that there are some concerns about the ideal quit date. Should it be during a particularly stressful time or a period of low stress? It doesn't matter. It will help, though, if you quit on a Friday. It will be a bonus if Friday precedes a long weekend.

This suggestion to quit on a Friday is not to avoid stressful situations over the weekend but to help you solidify the commitment to quit. Spend the weekend with your partner, family, and friends giving them your undivided attention for the first time in your adult life. Call your parents or your siblings if you haven't spoken to them for some time. Connect with your old friends on social media or even better call them. You don't have to talk to them about how or why you quit smoking. Just connect with them the way you used to before you took up smoking. They haven't seen the honest, calm, and relaxed you for a very long time.

Use a couple of hours to take stock of your counter-conditioning and stimulus control measures in the evenings and try to automate your new habits that will replace the costly and time-consuming habit of smoking.

But most importantly, use the time to heal. After quitting, you will feel the same sense of relief, accomplishment, and pride as the climber returning to the base camp after successfully summiting Mount Everest. But you have been drained, both mentally and physically, by years of smoking. Enjoy healthy meals, drink plenty of water, sleep in, and take an afternoon nap. Pamper yourself—you deserve it. If you have any passions that you have lost touch with, revisit them. Dig out your old record player from the back of the closet, dust off your guitar, or soften your old painting brushes (I hear vinegar is very effective on paintbrushes). Use the weekend to reinforce the things that fill your life with joy, and then on Sunday night, think about how smoking had robbed you of all the happiness in life. The first day back at work will be an exceptional experience. You will feel light and liberated. Enjoy every bit of it.

In any case, only pick the quit day after you have given the counter-conditioning and stimulus control plans a brief whirl. You want to iron out any wrinkles in your quit plan before taking the plunge. I set a calendar entry for a one-hour meeting with the nonsmoker me on my quit day. I wanted to spend the hour contemplating the life that lay ahead of me as a nonsmoker. I wanted to remind myself that what I had left behind was a path full of disappointments and regrets. I also wanted to tell the nonsmoker me that the next few weeks will be challenging, but I am in control of my life and should not allow a dirty, life-sucking cigarette to dictate how I use my time, health, and money.

But in reality, the quit day will set itself in most cases. You will instinctively realize the need to quit. As I was putting my plans to the test in my final quit attempt, I suddenly felt that I was ready to quit and put out my last cigarette, almost five days before my anticipated quit date. I had about half a pack of cigarettes left, which I doused in a wet ashtray. I felt that giving my left-over cigarettes to another smoker will not be doing them any good. Also, I didn't see any point in smoking till I ran out of the current pack. I saw it as my sunk cost and made no attempts to recover it.

Of course, I honored my meeting schedule with the nonsmoker me but well ahead of time. It felt different from all other failed quit attempts of the past. I did not have to make a promise of not smoking another cigarette in my life. I knew that I had put out the last cigarette that I ever smoked. I did not feel the need to announce my achievement to the world. I sat there, in my usual smoking spot at work, wondering how I had squandered my youth indulging in a stupid habit that was at best parasitic; it only took but never gave. Although I sat there quietly in contemplation, a part of me wanted to scream "freedom," like William Wallace (played by Mel Gibson) in the movie Braveheart. But I silenced my inner voice considering that the executioner was hacking Wallace's genitals with a blunt machete during his freedom cry.

Moving on from Scottish patriots and their hacked genitals, let's address the other concern surrounding the method of quitting—should you quit cold turkey or gradually reduce the number of cigarettes smoked every day and then quit?

Smokers who quit cold turkey draw a lot of skepticism from and sometimes envy of smokers. There are countless blogs and internet articles dedicated to informing their audiences that quitting cold turkey is difficult and has a poor success rate. Most websites and online testimonies attribute the ineffectiveness of the cold turkey method to the excessive use of willpower.

Consequently, most smokers fall for the misinformation about using willpower. The fact is this: quitting cold turkey involves abrupt cessation, and its counterpart requires the smoker to gradually cut down the number of cigarettes smoked per day (the gradual reduction method is also known as the cut-down method). Let's get realistic. Doesn't limiting the daily number of cigarettes involve the use of willpower? Of course, it does. The use of willpower is not limited to quitting cold turkey, and all methods available to assist quit smoking rely on willpower.

But is quitting cold turkey as ineffective as what we have come to believe? Let's evaluate the evidence for the success using the cold turkey method versus the gradual reduction method.

Most smokers who attempt to quit smoking do so cold turkey [142, 177-179]. A recent clinical study conducted by researchers at Oxford University and the University College London showed that abruptly quitting increases your chances of staying quit [180]. In this study, seven hundred long-term smokers were given behavioral support from nurses and used nicotine replacement. One group of participants quit abruptly, and the other group reduced the number of cigarettes by three-fourth over two weeks and then quit smoking. After four weeks of quitting, only 40 percent of the people who quit gradually remained smoke-free, but more than half of those who quit abruptly remained quit. Abstinence rates fell over the next six months, and many began to relapse. Only 15 percent of those who quit smoking gradually continued to abstain after six months, while almost a quarter of abrupt quitters remained smoke-free. The author attributed the lower success rates in those who quit gradually to difficulty in planning and poorer motivation [180]. In my opinion, people who attempt to quit gradually have not fully resolved their commitment to becoming a permanent nonsmoker. The cut-down method, however, has some utility. It can be useful for building motivation in smokers who have no intention to quit [181].

The clinical study conducted by researchers at Oxford University and the University College London is by no means the only large study to conclude on the superiority of quitting cold turkey. A major four-country study (the United Kingdom, the United States, Canada, and Australia) that surveyed thousands of smokers over three years showed that a quarter of those who used the cold turkey method successfully quit smoking compared with under 15 percent among those who used the cut-down method [178]. Abrupt quitters were also more likely to stay quit over fifteen months [178]. Surprisingly, heavy smokers were more likely to quit cold turkey [178].

Another large study that included data from over eight thousand adult Australians showed that almost 80 percent of smokers who quit cold turkey successfully quit smoking compared to 35 percent using nicotine replacement therapy [179]. At least three other clinical trials show that quitting cold turkey increasing your chances of quitting and staying quit [182]. Even the clinical practice guidelines of the U.S. Department of Health and Human Services mandates that clinicians advise their patients, who are willing to quit, to set a quit date within two weeks and abruptly quit [183]. The evidence is clear, and quitting cold turkey is currently the best choice to kick the habit.

But there is a catch with quitting cold turkey. It works better in people who have stronger motivations and determination to quit [180, 184]. There is evidence to show that quitting cold turkey is five times better in achieving a longer quit duration than nicotine patches or varenicline (a drug used to treat nicotine addiction) when motivation is particularly strong such as a severe health condition [185]. I am sure this fact is not surprising for most smokers, but it is an important fact. We have already discussed motivation and determination at length, and by now, I am sure that you understand the difference between wanting to quit and being determined to quit. There is good evidence that you are more likely to quit smoking successfully if you have a serious intention to quit and believe that quitting is possible [186]. If you are genuinely motivated to quit, your willpower will also serve you longer. Researchers from the University at Albany, have shown that willpower lasts longer in people who are motivated to do the given task even if it is a difficult task [187, 188].

A common misconception with the terms *cold-turkey* or *abrupt quitting* is that they imply an unplanned quit attempt [189]. Quitting cold turkey, by definition, does not require the smoker to cut down on cigarettes gradually. But abruptly quitting *can be* and *must be* planned. The clinical trial from Oxford University and the University College London discussed above-instructed participants to identify cues, time of the day when the urge to smoke was the strongest, and plan strategies to prevent relapse after the quit day [180]. The latest research from my research group also suggests that over two-thirds of smokers who quit cold turkey actively search for information on the internet to create a quit plan.

Chapter Summary

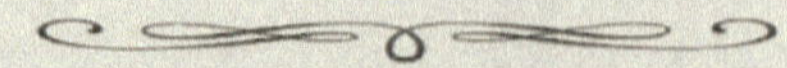

✓ Quit at any time of the year. Life isn't going to get any simpler than it already is!

✓ Test your strategies for staying quit before setting a quit date.

✓ Quitting on a Friday will give you some time off so that you can engage in the process of healing and reconnecting with things in life that brings you joy.

✓ Quitting cold turkey is the best way to stop smoking.

Maintenance: Implementing your counter-conditioning and stimulus control plans

Maintaining peace can be as strenuous as winning a war.

-Margaret MacMillan, historian and professor at the University of Oxford

Remember the mantra from my friend Li: *Quitting smoking is easy; staying quit is hard.* If you have been smoking for several years, cigarettes have become an integral part of your life. As a result, the last cigarette that you smoke will create a rather large void in your life. You will have more time and energy than you have ever known. Not knowing what to do with this superfluous time and energy is a big part of the withdrawal symptoms and the real cause of the persistent itch that all quitters report. This itch causes greater impulsivity and, ultimately, relapse [190].

The counter-conditioning and the stimulus control strategies that you test during the experimentation stage will be useful in filling the void created by cigarettes. But just after a few days, you will realize that quitting has a far more significant impact on your lifestyle than you could imagine.

You will be achieving greater concentration, productivity, fitness, and will have the libido of an Emperor Penguin. And you know what? You will still have some time left to fill and energy to spare. Please be aware of this when it happens and take a minute to contemplate. The awareness of these positive changes will help you realize how much smoking was costing you. To give you an idea, I was consistently running a total of fifty kilometers every week after just three months of quitting. I ran my first ever marathon after six months. I authored twelve scientific papers and four books in the two years after quitting smoking. All of this with a high teaching load at the university. I still had enough time to be an active and involved father and husband at home.

But about a year after I quit smoking, my body was unable to cope with the increased levels of both mental and physical fitness, and I started feeling very tired. Since I was enjoying one of my most productive periods at work, I decided to scale down my runs by half. Over time, I learned to use different techniques on weeks that are physically or mentally demanding. During weeks that were physically demanding, I scaled down my runs but added lighter activities such as spending extra time reading a book or building train models with my daughter. I incorporated more physical activity during weeks when I was consumed by writing academic papers and books. Such fine-tunings will be necessary as you continue to adjust to the life of a nonsmoker.

A friend of mine, also a professor, who was one of the early readers of this book, took up running a week before quitting and scaled up his weekly mileage during the first month of becoming a nonsmoker. Just like me, he realized that his creativity and productivity went through the roof and was fully engaged in teaching and research. Running, as a counter-conditioning technique, was no longer feasible for him. He briefly flirted with the prospects of weekend hiking and cycling, decided that it was not for him, and ultimately joined a gym where he now spends three days a week.

Until you are confident of your permanent escape from the cycle of quitting and relapse, devote at least ten minutes at the end of each week to review your resolve toward staying smoke-free. If you like to be very organized or have a hectic weekly schedule, I suggest that you set a ten minutes calendar block that automatically repeats at a set time and day of the week. Use this time to review your counter-conditioning and stimulus control techniques. Ensure that you are not pushing yourself too hard. Otherwise, experiment with new coping mechanisms that match your changing lifestyle. You can always return to this book and reread the sections on counter-conditioning and stimulus control to refresh your understanding. In any case, keep your counter-conditioning and stimulus control techniques as dynamic as possible and adapt quickly to the positive changes in your life.

Dealing with withdrawal symptoms

The number and severity of withdrawal symptoms depend on your mindset. As discussed in the preceding chapters, there is no underlying basis for experiencing withdrawal symptoms because you are not addicted to nicotine. It is part of the nocebo effect of smoking cessation. If you quit smoking as I have, fully realizing that you are not addicted, your withdrawal symptoms will be mild. I was restless for a few days after quitting and did not experience any of the *common withdrawal symptoms* [fn21]. Each episode of restlessness lasted for less than a minute, and I experienced this three to five times a day for about a week.

Even if you experience withdrawal symptoms, they are signs that your body functions are returning to normal (e.g., better appetite, increased thirst, and sleepiness at odd times), or your brain is seeking reward (e.g., low mood or restlessness). In almost all cases, withdrawal symptoms peak around the third day and will begin to subside immediately after [191].

Normalizing your bodily functions and your brain seeking reward are both positive and necessary processes. Years of smoking have damaged virtually all parts of your body, and the repair process starts immediately after you quit. Eating nutritious food, drinking plenty of water, and

---

[fn21] Common withdrawal symptoms can include irritability, anger, frustration, anxiety, depressed mood, difficulty concentrating, increased appetite, restlessness, and insomnia [14, 191]. Withdrawal symptoms are so overrated that the most appropriate place to include this information is here, as a minor footnote.

catching up on some extra sleep over the first three days will help the healing process.

Moreover, since so many of your experiences were built around smoking, it is natural for the brain to seek rewards when cigarettes become as irrelevant as a peephole on a glass door. We are creatures of habit after all, and quitting creates a rather large void leaving the brain craving for more reward. I was restless for the first few days after quitting because I did not know what to do with the extra time and energy I had as a nonsmoker. This state was unusual enough for my brain to take notice. Smoking had taken much of my time and energy for sixteen years, and busy and tired had become the norm.

This is where counter-conditioning plans that are in themselves rewarding will become useful. Don't resist when the brain craves a reward. Give it any rewarding experience that does not involve cigarettes. All the counter-conditioning and stimulus control plans that I have described in this book (exercise, reading, financial planning, and eating nutritious food) are rewarding. You can minimize or even eliminate all withdrawal symptoms using these simple strategies.

I think some of you may find a couple of other strategies that I used in my past quit attempts useful—victory counting and journaling. I did not use these strategies as much in the final quit attempt but used them extensively in earlier attempts. I experienced more intense withdrawal symptoms during my past quit attempts, such as restlessness, low mood, and insomnia. Although the quit attempts were ultimately unsuccessful, the strategies were effective in keeping my motivation high and keeping my smoker's brain from exaggerating the situation.

Victory counting involves counting the number of opportunities where you could have had a cigarette if you wanted to but didn't. Here is my victory count routine for today: the first opportunity to buy and smoke cigarettes was as I cycled past my favorite smoking spot, which is a small enclosed area on the way to the university with vending machines for cigarettes and coffee. The area is very quiet in the morning and used to be a perfect place to plan my day with coffee and cigarettes. The second opportunity I had was a minute later when I rode past the convenience store where five or six people, probably in their early 20s, thronged around the ashtray like a pack of wolves around a dead rhinoceros. I rode past three other convenient stores before I reached work (convenience stores are far too many in Japan). During lunch, I went to a nearby convenience store to grab a quick bite. After work, I met a friend—a veteran smoker—for coffee. That was a total of seven opportunities. I imagine a scoreboard ticking every time I forego an opportunity—Me: 7, Cigarettes: 0. The brain perceives each forgone opportunity as a victory and gives itself a dopamine rush. But the reason I enjoy this exercise so much is that it reminds me who the boss really is. I am no longer a slave and am in full control of my life. I do victory counting institutively every once in a while, and it still feels good.

The second strategy that I used is far less original and is widely used in behavioral therapy—journaling. I used journaling in my last failed quit attempt and the final successful attempt for about a month after quitting smoking. In both cases, I reviewed and recorded every smoking-related detail of the previous day in my note-keeping app. I noted all cravings with situational context. I also wrote about how I prevailed in certain situations. The goal was to track successes (for positive reinforcement) and identify triggers. The written record prevented my brain from concocting a story or exaggerate the severity of the situation. As smokers, we have learned to do both.

Journaling every morning made me realize that quitting was not only possible, but it was also incredibly easy. I didn't die because of not smoking, and didn't kill anybody or throw a temper tantrum either. I could see past the stereotype. I had a more positive outlook on life and could see improvements in my creativity or productivity after just a few days. Even the way I described my experience changed quickly. In the first few days, I recorded any desire to smoke as "*cravings*" then as "*urges*" and after eight days or so consistently as "*passing thought that lasted less than a second.*" Many of my journal entries were a single sentence (e.g., "*Day 11: Yesterday was perfect—no cravings*"), and others (such as the entry about the three angels of Kahneman) were longer. I had no idea then that these written records of my post-quitting experience will be the most valuable asset while writing this book.

Coping with stress

Considering all that we have discussed so far about smoking and stress, it should come as no surprise that *quitting smoking will reduce your stress levels*. At least thirty scientific studies show that anxiety, depression, and stress decreases after quitting smoking [192-195]. People who quit smoking as a result of behavioral change without using any nicotine replacement therapy have even lower stress, depression, and anxiety compared to those who quit using nicotine replacement therapy [194].

This decrease in your stress level after post-quitting should help you deal with most stressful situations better. But the problem is that smokers have learned to deal with minor inconveniences of life, major stressors, and everything in between with cigarettes. As a nonsmoker, you will re-experience all the minor inconveniences as well as major stressors and will learn to differentiate the two. Most smokers are oblivious to the fact that minor inconveniences of life and major stressors do not require equally high priority response. In time, you will learn to cope with both situations appropriately.

I remember how emails and phone calls consumed a huge amount of my time and used to stress me out. Fortunately, I am not as neurotic as I use to be back then. I now return all my emails in a batch on Friday afternoons. Also, my work emails have an automatic postscript: *"I only respond to emails on Friday so that I can focus on cutting-edge research and writing papers. If the matter is urgent, please call me on my desk phone."* Even the dean cannot argue with such a postscript. He hired me based on my research and an excellent publication record. I think this is the most appropriate response to anything that is a minor inconvenience. Also, only my family and close friends get on-demand access to me on my cellphone. Everyone else can wait until I have nothing better to do.

I also feel ready to take on any major stressors that come my way as I am now physically and mentally fitter, productive, creative, and financially secure. In the interest of full disclosure, I have not been able to test the effect of quit smoking on major stressors. I have not experienced any major stressors since becoming a nonsmoker. I enjoy my work, my wife and I rarely have any arguments, and I enjoy the time with our mischievous eighteen-months-old daughter. Nimisha can be annoying at times, but she never stresses me out. I can see the innocence in her actions. When she breaks something in the house or jumps off the bed, I understand that she has no way of knowing that it is an expensive vase or things will break when smashed against a brick wall or a concrete floor. She is exploring her environment the way she should. Everybody who has known me since I started wearing my underpants the right way knows that this is the calmest I have ever been.

If you think that these positive changes, especially coping with stresses and inconveniences, take months after quitting, you are in for yet another surprise. It takes just a few weeks for newer coping mechanisms to develop. The few weeks is to allow you to re-experience a variety of minor inconveniences of life as well as some major stressors. In reality, you only need to experience a situation once, and your brain will learn to cope with the stress on its own without craving a cigarette. It sounds too easy because it is. Smoking never helped you solve any of your problems, and removing cigarettes from the equation does not change a thing. It was always you solving problems, and it still is just you solving the problem. You have removed an irrelevant factor from the equation. Smoking always was a bystander in all our experiences, and we raised it to superhero status. It never de-stressed us or made us braver. If anything, cigarettes made us afraid of not being able to survive without it.

So, until you re-experience a variety of minor inconveniences and major stressors, implement your stimulus control strategies rigorously. Identify the irrelevant, avoidable, and workable stimuli that may bring back the urge to smoke. Forget the irrelevant ones, avoid any stimulus that has little room in your new life as a nonsmoker, and put extra effort on the rest. After about two or three weeks, you will be able to stand naked in a room full of smokers without the slightest urge to smoke.

I must warn you of a few things that increase your risk of relapse. First, you cannot stand in a room full of smokers naked without convincing them and yourself that quitting makes people nutty as a fruitcake. So, don't go bonkers. Second, if a very close family or a friend is a smoker, you will find it incredibly tempting to light a cigarette. Most people relapse this way. The best way to address the problem will be to turn into a quit smoking advocate with the best intentions of your loved ones. Talk to them about how smoking is an irrational act, why quitting is the sensible thing to do, the marvelous positive changes in your life, and how easy it was for you to quit smoking. This will further reinforce your commitment to staying quit. Your loved ones may respond in two possible ways. They may quit because of your pestering, and you both can feel good about it. Or they will stop smoking in your presence. Either way, you come out the winner.

And an equally important third is the use of alcohol. Alcohol removes inhibitions, and when drinking, you will have to be extra vigilant not to fall for the "just one cigarette" argument. Remember that the years of enslavement to smoking was because of just one cigarette. In the first three weeks after quitting, I suggest that you don't drink at all. If this is not possible for whatever reason, at least avoid drinking in the company of other smokers. I guesstimate that almost 80 percent of my effort in stimulus control has been around alcohol (The stereotype, in this case, maybe true: academics tend to be borderline alcoholics.)

I enjoy drinking beer, especially during the summer months, because it feels refreshing on a hot day. Although I recognized drinking as a major trigger, I did not have to (or want to) become a teetotaller when I quit smoking. I only had to be a bit more vigilant, and alternating glasses of water between drinks helped. But I am no longer worried about alcohol triggering any urge to smoke; cigarettes are not served chilled or modify the taste of beer, and therefore cannot possibly add to the refreshing experience on a hot summer day. The desire to drink and then reinforce the pleasure with cigarettes is long dead. If you enjoy drinking, you will have to learn to dissociate smoking from alcohol, enjoyment, and celebration.

Envision any stressful situations and smoking triggers and visualize them as discussed under *Experimentation.* Make sure to thoroughly evaluate both your coping mechanisms, including counter-conditioning and stimulus control plans, when the ten-minute weekly meeting reminder pops up.

Manage your weight

My experience as a smoker, those of others I have had the opportunity to help, and the scientific evidence all indicate that with a good understanding of smoking behavior and effective strategies for staying quit, withdrawal symptoms and coping with stress are not significant issues post-quitting. For this reason, I only briefly dealt with post-quitting withdrawal symptoms and stress in this chapter. The subject of weight gain, however, is different in that both experience and evidence indicate that it is a real issue. Combined results from over sixty studies indicate that quitters can gain anywhere between one and five kilograms in the first year [196, 197]. Many smokers do not wish to quit because of the fear of weight gain.

Smoking induces an anorexia-like state and suppresses appetite [198]. After you quit smoking, your appetite will rapidly recover. The normalizing of appetite is a positive sign that your body is repairing itself. But two other changes in eating behavior post-quitting makes the normalizing of a smoker's appetite a Trojan horse. First, your taste buds start to recover from the onslaught of seven thousand chemicals soon after you quit smoking [199-201]. Naturally, better-tasting food in more appetizing, and the concept of portion control goes down the tubes. Second, many quitters use high-calorie food such as candies, chocolates, and chips as a counter-conditioning technique. Convenience food, which is almost always calorie-dense, apparently helps to mimic the hand-to-mouth motion of smoking. The triple threat presented by increased appetite, return of taste buds, and people resorting to junk food to cope with cravings are a surefire way to turn anyone into a blue whale.

I have already addressed the problem of inappropriate coping behavior after quitting while discussing counter-conditioning strategies. But this warrants more discussion here in the specific context of weight gain.

It is important to remember two facts through all stages of the quit smoking process. First, quitting smoking doesn't make you hungrier; it only normalizes your appetite. There is no need to increase your food intake. Second, using calorie-dense food to mimic the hand-to-mouth motion of smoking does not break the habit of smoking. Instead, you are creating a new unhealthy habit of snacking while retaining the one you are trying to break. Like I said before, replacing the usual action (smoking) with another action (snacking) to a particular trigger will not provide the same rewarding experience. Instead, you need to suppress the old habit of smoking with another emotionally stronger habit altogether.

As discussed in earlier chapters, the necessary criteria for a good counter-conditioning technique are:

- Must not produce any negative effects such as weight gain.

- Must make the gains in the primary motivators (money, health, and time) after quitting immediately observable.

- Must have a greater emotional appeal than cigarettes. This criterion excludes most consumer products.

- Must be easy to do, inexpensive, and sustainable for at least two years.

High-calorie food breaks all the criteria for a good counter-conditioning technique except being easy. Therefore, using food, or for that matter, any other substitute, to cope with the void created by smoking guarantees a relapse. Substitute, by definition, works both ways. You can substitute cigarettes with food, and before you know it, you will be substituting food with cigarettes again. It simply does not work. Therefore, you should not aim to replace smoking with anything. You need to create an emotionally appealing goal such as a healthy lifestyle, financial independence, or being a better role model for your children that do not seek to replace any aspect of your smoking habit. Quitting smoking becomes essential to achieving your emotionally charged goals.

If you fear weight gain after quitting, I strongly recommend that you include at least one physical activity as a counter-conditioning and stimulus control techniques. I incorporated running and walking into my daily routine and as a result, lost fourteen kilograms in the first year of quitting smoking. I was also eating healthier, which further assisted my weight loss. Now, physical activity and healthy eating are a natural part of my life and require minimal effort. You have a variety of physical activities to choose from: running, walking, hiking, cycling, yoga, pilates, dancing, or just simple strategies like taking the stairs instead of escalators and elevators can work in your favor. If you have the luxury of time and can afford a gym membership go for it, but only if you feel you can maintain the interest and motivation to sustain this habit. It is always safer to choose a simple form of physical activity and not an exotic one. Exotic exercises such as Zumba dance workout or hula hooping are great, but when the hype and novelty surrounding such activities fade, you will lose the motivation to continue.

Of course, you also need to watch what you eat. The problem is that nutritional science is currently at a stage where you can find a conflicting "expert opinion" for virtually any advice. We don't have to micromanage our diets and focus on every single nutrient known to humankind. We need to zoom out and start focusing on whole, nutritious food. So here is a zoomed out advice: if your grandparents ate it, it is generally OK for you to eat; if you did not have the opportunity to observe your grandparent's diet then eat the food that looks like it came from a farm and pass on the food that looks like it came from a factory. The following food recommendation chart, also based on my zoomed-out view of nutrition, is simple, easy to remember, and will help you make better food choices.

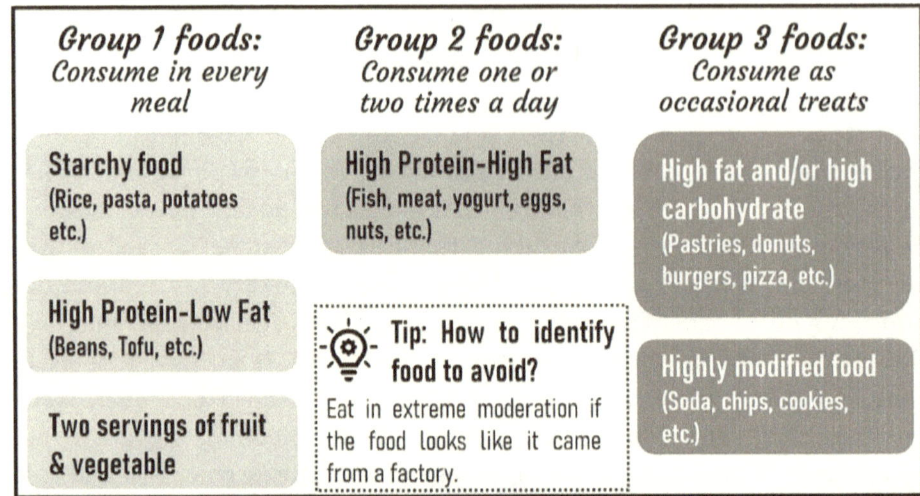

After you quit smoking, it will be particularly important to avoid food rich in fat and carbohydrates and consume more protein and fiber-rich food. Unlike fat and carbohydrate, proteins make you feel fuller for longer and increase muscle mass [202]. Also, proteins have the same calorie as carbohydrates but half as much as fat. Eggs, meat, yogurt, tofu, and cheese are excellent sources of protein.

Unlike fat, carbohydrate, and proteins, fibers contain zero calories but have three vital functions related to weight loss. First, fibers absorb water in the intestine, swells, and makes you feel fuller. Second, fibers help in the digestion of food. But certain food, especially calorie-rich fluids such as juice or soda and highly processed food such as pastries or candies, require very little digestion, and the calories are rapidly absorbed from the intestines. Calories that enter your bloodstream quickly and cause a massive increase in blood sugar levels are the ones that ultimately cause type 2 diabetes and obesity. This is where the third and perhaps the most important function of dietary fibers come into play. Dietary fibers slow down the rate at which calories enter your bloodstream from the intestines and therefore prevent the sudden and massive rise in blood sugar levels. Any plant-based food (except processed grains such as polished rice and white flour) is a good source of fiber.

Remember that the idea is not to eliminate carbohydrates or fat—they are both essential, and neither is bad. If you are consuming any natural or minimally processed food, you will be ingesting all three macronutrients in proportions that your body has evolved to digest and metabolize efficiently. The problem with processed food is that the proportion of the three macronutrients is modified; they contain too much of one nutrient and too little of others. The more processed food you consume, the more difficult it will be to maintain a balanced diet that contains good proportions of carbohydrate, fat, and protein. It is this skewed nutrient composition that is bad for the waistline. For example, foods such as bread, cookies, cakes, pastries, and pies—delicious as they are—have excess carbohydrates or fat and almost no protein. Oil is an extreme example of processed food. It is entirely made up of one nutrient, fat, and devoid of any carbohydrate or protein. Table sugar is another example, entirely made up of carbohydrates. Can you think of any natural food that is wholly made up of one nutrient? Nature did not intend for us to eat just one macronutrient and highly refined food, of which oil and sugar are the ultimate forms, makes eating a balanced diet very difficult, if not impossible. Another problem with processed food is that it is completely stripped of micronutrients (vitamins, minerals, and fiber).

Fat and carbohydrates are more abundant in our food, both natural or processed, than protein. The best source of protein (meat, eggs, beans, nuts, milk, cheese, yogurt, and tofu) contains at most 30 percent protein, and the rest of it is fat and carbohydrate. As a result of this protein intake is often not adequate in the general population. So instead of planning your food around carbohydrates sources such as rice and bread, plan it around food rich in protein such as a grilled steak or bean salad.

Sometimes food choices can be confusing as most foods have all three macronutrients. In such cases, I use the following simple rules of thumb:

- As much as possible, avoid industrially processed food.

- Prioritize protein over fat and carbohydrates.

- Carbohydrates should get the lowest preference as it is the most abundant nutrient.

- Prefer small amounts of protein-fat combinations (e.g., grilled meat, yogurt) over fat-carbohydrates combinations (e.g., cookies, cakes, and chocolates).

- Fruits are an exception to carbohydrate rule. Nature has nicely packed fruits with water, vitamins, minerals, and fiber.

But the most important nutrient you should be paying attention to is water. It is the weak link in any quit smoking plan because of the way our brain differentiates—or more accurately cannot differentiate—the cravings for cigarettes, food, and water. Hypothalamus, the command center of the brain that manages our stress system and is hijacked by smoking, also senses hunger and thirst, and plays a vital role in long-term weight change [203]. Consequently, the cravings for cigarettes are indistinguishable from those for food and water. As if that was not complicated enough, years of smoking make the hypothalamus more responsiveness to food, thereby making it the preferred source of instant gratification [203]. You are more likely to reach for food when you feel hungry, thirsty, or want to smoke a cigarette. This is yet another reason for post-quitting weight gain.

After you quit smoking, it will be easy for you to identify the craving for cigarettes. Smoking is a habit, and like most habits, it is linked with time, people, place, or things—the cues. By simple deduction, any craving in the presence of a familiar cue must be because of not smoking. We have also discussed several ways to manage the triggers for smoking. This should take care of the craving for cigarettes, which will be gone in a few days anyway.

You can easily avoid the craving for water by making sure you are well hydrated, a state you should always try to be in. Dehydration can cause depressed mood, fatigue, and decreased alertness [204], all of which can make relapsing easier. Don't confuse yourself with the recommended intake and if the recommended intake includes water in food or not. I find most national dietary recommendations impractical because most people cannot follow the advice with the same scientific precision. For instance, most dietary recommendations suggest that 60 percent of your calories should come from carbohydrates. Even the people who wrote that recommendation will have a hard time figuring out what 60 percent of the calories from carbohydrates will look like on a dinner plate. The recommendations for water are far more inconsistent and confusing. My suggestion to keep hydrated is this: buy a one-liter water bottle (32 Oz), and remember to refill it once after lunch. Smaller bottles are convenient to carry, but you will have to remember to refill it more often.

Once you eliminate the cravings for cigarettes and water, any remaining craving means that you are hungry, and it is time to supply your body with nutritious food rich in proteins and fibers. Most vitamins and minerals are required in small amounts, and consuming a variety of natural food often takes care of these aptly named *micro*nutrients without any fuss. Now that you have learned how to isolate your hunger pangs, you will also not feel the need to snack as often.

Chapter Summary

- ✓ You can expect dramatic changes in your lifestyle after quitting. You must adapt quickly to changes.

- ✓ Review your counter-conditioning and stimulus control strategies at least once a week to ensure you are at the top of your game.

- ✓ If any, withdrawal symptoms are generally mild. Do not overthink this and work on managing any symptoms that you may experience.

- ✓ In any case, withdrawal symptoms subside after three days.

- ✓ Contrary to what you may think, your stress levels will decrease after quitting. You will get better at handling other stressors and inconveniences of life.

- ✓ Alcohol and a smoker in your family or friends circle pose the greatest threat to your status of being a nonsmoker. Plan to deal with them before quitting.

- ✓ The risk of weight gain is real but can be easily managed by diet tracking and exercise as a part of your counter-conditioning plan.

The final exit

*I'm more proud of quitting smoking than of anything
else I've done in my life, including winning an Oscar.*

-Christine Lahti, actress and filmmaker

*I*sn't it amazing how a group of people glamourized smoking, another group demonized it, and after almost two centuries of misinformation, we as a society believe both sides of the story? We started smoking, thinking that it makes us brave, cool, sophisticated, and socially desirable. After a few years, we convince ourselves that we are addicted to a specific chemical in tobacco smoke, and pinning it on one out of the seven thousand chemicals gives it an aura of surety. We fall deeper into the deception and believe that smoking relieves our stress, makes us productive, and quitting will cause severe withdrawal symptoms.

The anti-smoking campaign (the message of which is essentially *quit smoking or else*) accentuates the power of the deception by instilling fear. Like stress and smoking, fear suppresses the prefrontal cortex impairing our rationality and impulse-control behavior. Consider the following scenario. Bob, the smoker from the chapter on determination, is back again, and this time he is convinced by the doom and gloom campaign that smoking causes cancer. The message is correct; smoking causes cancer, among other things. Bob is sacred to his bones that he may someday develop painful cancer. This fear motivates him to quit smoking, but Bob soon realizes that quitting is easier said than done. He relapses and accepts that escape is impossible. Understandably, Bob feels he is addicted beyond redemption. If the fear of horrendous pain and suffering of cancer and chemotherapy—or worst, death—can not get him to quit smoking, nothing can. Ultimately, Bob believes, without a scintilla of doubt, that he is addicted to cigarettes and is a confirmed smoker. This deadly combination of deception and fear convinces the smoker that escape is impossible.

Years of smoking and fear of death has suppressed Bob's rationality to the extent that he does not consider if the failed quit attempt was the result of addressing the wrong problem. The question that drove Bob to try and quit smoking was, *"what smoking does TO my body?"* This is the wrong question to ask because most smokers do not light the first cigarettes hoping the act does something to their body. I say most people because my friend Jessica took to smoking to maintain a slim figure. But smoking certainly doesn't make Bob high, numb, or give him a tingling sensation that he happens to enjoy. In comparison, cocaine, heroin, or alcohol abusers are charmed by the intoxicating effects of their preferred drug on their bodies. Most smokers start smoking cigarettes as a social prop and never really think of what smoking does to their body. If the effect of smoking on the body was never a motivation to start smoking, it also could not be the motivation to quit.

Instead, the right question to ask is, *"what smoking does FOR me?"* This is the real reason why we started smoking: we believed that smoking made us look cool, brave, and sophisticated. Later we believed that smoking relieves our stress and makes us productive. We now know that none of this is true, and smoking does absolutely nothing for us! If anything, smoking causes stress and robs you of your creativity and productivity. Smoking does not help you make friends; it limits your social circle. And cigarette is not your friend, for crying out loud!

Much of our reality depends on how we view things. I concede that we, as smokers, had no way of knowing any of the fallacies when we smoked the first cigarette. We had not seen the scientific evidence that nicotine in cigarettes does not cause addiction, and there will be no terrible withdrawal symptoms. But now you have seen the evidence. Moreover, you now fully realize exactly how much you pay for smoking with your money, health, and time, and receive nothing in return, not even a buzz. Once your mind sees smoking for what it truly is—a habit with no potential upside—quitting becomes an easy process for your body.

Allow me to indulge in the extra salesmanship one last time and remind you of the amazing benefits of quitting. As a nonsmoker, even simple things in life will start to feel different. Do you remember, from before becoming a smoker, what it felt like to breathe the freshness of the morning air? How eating was not just stuffing food into your mouth, but you also used your sense of sight and smell to enjoy the food? Do you remember the time when it was possible to talk to someone without worrying about your foul breath or the smell of burned tobacco emanating from your hair and clothes? And do you recall how easy and enjoyable it was to walk and run around without being out of breath? If your memory is hazy, that's OK; you are now ready to rediscover a life full of possibilities without constant interruptions to smoke another filthy cigarette. You will also find out, for the first time, how liberating it is to walk around without a pack of cigarettes in your pocket, not having to constantly seek an opportunity to smoke, or worrying if you have the stock to last you the night. You are about to gain full control of your money, health, and time and it is not going to cost a dime. All you must do is remain honest, mindful, and take baby steps to enjoy your freedom.

As we part ways, let me leave you with a quote from Norman Vincent Peale that replaced Li's quote on my desk and my smartphone's lock screen a few days after I quit smoking: *"Throw your heart over the bar, and your body will follow."* These simple eleven words accurately capture the most important lesson I learned from my quit smoking experience.

Gratitude, apologies, and a time capsule.

I want to start by thanking Dr. Bibechana Timsina for being my first reader, critic, proof-reader, motivator-in-chief, and a wonderful wife. On the one hand, your opinions and ideas were a constant reminder that this book is not a research paper or an academic book. Instead, it is for people from all walks of life who are struggling to quit smoking and can benefit from my experience and expertise. On the other hand—the wife's hand— your love and care is what made quitting smoking a walk in the park for me and writing this book a possibility.

A big thank you to Dr. Saeed Idrees, Dr. Nikan Sadehvandi, and Dr. Zi Peng Li for your insights into the minds of a smoker. Your contribution was essential for the ideas to crystallize in my mind. Also, many thanks to my research students for digging out hundreds of research articles on smoking. It was a lot of material, and your efforts helped make this book an exhaustive compendium of evidence.

I must also take this opportunity to thank a few people who are as aware of my existence as I am of deep-sea creatures. Although the vastness of space and time separates us, they have spoken to me and inspired me through the pages of their books. I would like to thank the following individuals (in no particular order): Napoleon Hill, Robert Kiyosaki, Joshua Fields Millburn and Ryan Nicodemus from The Minimalists, Malcolm Gladwell, Greg Mckeown, Richie Norton, Cal Newport, Steven D. Levitt, Stephen J. Dubner, Daniel Kahneman, T. Colin Campbell, Viktor E Frankl, Harper Lee, Stephen King, Spencer Johnson, Mark Manson, E.B White, and the fantastic Randy Pausch.

As I write this part, I feel more repentant than grateful. I want to apologize to my parents, sister, wife, and daughter for not giving you my undivided attention and, most importantly, for being dishonest (I may have sneaked out once or twice making an insane sounding excuse). By the time I quit smoking in 2016, I had squandered away a fortune on smoking. A part of that fortune was not mine to squander, and for this, I must apologize to my parents.

Finally, my sincere apology to every person who had to unwilling inhale my secondhand smoke—you did not deserve to be put at risk. To the best of my knowledge, I have not inspired anyone to take up smoking. But the chances are that I am wrong. I hope that this book reaches out to those who took up smoking on my account and that you will accept my heartfelt apologies for not being the role model you deserved.

Now to the time capsule part of things. I want to leave a message for our beautiful daughter Nimisha Sayuri Poudyal here, in the first edition of this book. I wish you could understand just how much you have inspired us to be better human beings, but I am sure you will know in time. One of my main inspirations for writing this book is you. Your mother and I intend to raise you, respecting your opinion and freewill. If someday you decide to take up smoking like your old man, that's your choice (although I already sense that you are way smarter than I am). But if you need a way out, I hope this book will help even in my absence. I have only two regrets in life. The first that I ever smoked and second, I didn't learn about money mechanics soon enough. I hope that you will have neither.

References

∞ ∞ ∞

Notes on using this reference list

All references to journal articles follow the format of [Authors.(Year) Article title. *Abbreviated Journal Name.* Volume, page numbers.]. The easiest way to find these articles is by searching using the article title on the internet. Although all articles cited here are available from the internet, some may require an active subscription to access full text. In such cases, full text of the article can also be obtained by contacting one of the authors by email. Sources that are not journal articles such as reports from World Health Organization and U.S. Department of Health and Human Services or book are accompanied by an URL.

∞ ∞ ∞

[1] Barnes, J.; Dong, C. Y., *et al.* (**2010**). Hypnotherapy for smoking cessation. *Cochrane Database Syst Rev*, -(Issue 10), CD001008.

[2] Keogan, S.; Li, S., *et al.* (**2019**). Allen Carr's Easyway to Stop Smoking - A randomised clinical trial. *Tob Control*, 28, 414-9.

[3] Dijkstra, A.; Zuidema, R., *et al.* (**2014**). The effectiveness of the Allen Carr smoking cessation training in companies tested in a quasi-experimental design. *BMC Public Health*, 14, 952.

[4] Foshee, J. P.; Oh, A., *et al.* (**2017**). Prospective, randomized, controlled trial using best-selling smoking-cessation book. *Ear Nose Throat J*, 96, 258-62.

[5] Henningfield, J. E.; Cohen, C., *et al.* (**1991**). Is nicotine more addictive than cocaine? *Br J Addict*, 86, 565-9.

[6] Frenk, H. and Dar, R. (**2011**). If the data contradict the theory, throw out the data: Nicotine addiction in the 2010 report of the Surgeon General. *Harm Reduct J*, 8, 12.

[7] Grant, J. E.; Potenza, M. N., *et al.* (**2010**). Introduction to behavioral addictions. *Am J Drug Alcohol Abuse*, 36, 233-41.

[8] U.S. Department of Health and Human Services (**2016**). Facing addiction in America: The Surgeon General's report on alcohol, drugs, and health. https://addiction.surgeongeneral.gov/sites/default/files/surgeon-generals-report.pdf

[9] Graybiel, A. M. (**2008**). Habits, rituals, and the evaluative brain. *Annu Rev Neurosci*, 31, 359-87.

[10] U.S. Department of Health and Human Services (**1988**). The health consequences of smoking: Nicotine addiction: A report of the surgeon general. https://profiles.nlm.nih.gov/NN/B/B/Z/D/

[11] Vigen, T. Spurious correlations. http://www.tylervigen.com/spurious-correlations

[12] Heatherton, T. F.; Kozlowski, L. T., *et al.* (**1991**). The Fagerstrom Test for Nicotine Dependence: a revision of the Fagerstrom Tolerance Questionnaire. *Br J Addict*, 86, 1119-27.

[13] Lairson, D. R.; Harrist, R., *et al.* (**1992**). Screening for patients with alcohol problems: severity of patients identified by the CAGE. *J Drug Educ*, 22, 337-52.

[14] American Psychiatric Association (**2013**). Diagnostic and statistical manual of mental disorders, fifth edition. https://dsm.psychiatryonline.org/doi/book/10.1176/appi.books.9780890425596

[15] Rodgman, A. and Perfetti, T. A. The Chemical Components of Tobacco and Tobacco Smoke: Boca Raton: CRC Press; **2013**. https://www.crcpress.com/The-Chemical-Components-of-Tobacco-and-Tobacco-Smoke-Second-Edition/Rodgman-Perfetti/p/book/9781466515482

[16] Taghavi, S.; Khashyarmanesh, Z., *et al.* (**2012**). Nicotine content of domestic cigarettes, imported cigarettes and pipe tobacco in iran. *Addict Health*, 4, 28-35.

[17] Korte, K. J.; Capron, D. W., *et al.* (**2013**). The Fagerstrom test for nicotine dependence: do revisions in the item scoring enhance the psychometric properties? *Addict Behav*, 38, 1757-63.

[18] Rose, J. E.; Behm, F. M., *et al.* (**2000**). Dissociating nicotine and nonnicotine components of cigarette smoking. *Pharmacol Biochem Behav*, 67, 71-81.

[19] Domino, E. F.; Ni, L., *et al.* (**2013**). Denicotinized versus average nicotine tobacco cigarette smoking differentially releases striatal dopamine. *Nicotine Tob Res*, 15, 11-21.

[20] Brody, A. L.; Mandelkern, M. A., *et al.* (**2009**). Ventral striatal dopamine release in response to smoking a regular vs a denicotinized cigarette. *Neuropsychopharmacology*, 34, 282-9.

[21] Rezaishiraz, H.; Hyland, A., *et al.* (**2007**). Treating smokers before the quit date: can nicotine patches and denicotinized cigarettes reduce cravings? *Nicotine Tob Res*, 9, 1139-46.

[22] Barrett, S. P. and Darredeau, C. (**2012**). The acute effects of nicotine on the subjective and behavioural responses to denicotinized tobacco in dependent smokers. *Behav Pharmacol*, 23, 221-7.

[23] Barrett, S. P. (**2010**). The effects of nicotine, denicotinized tobacco, and nicotine-containing tobacco on cigarette craving, withdrawal, and self-administration in male and female smokers. *Behav Pharmacol*, 21, 144-52.

[24] Addicott, M. A.; Froeliger, B., *et al.* (**2014**). Nicotine and non-nicotine smoking factors differentially modulate craving, withdrawal and cerebral blood flow as measured with arterial spin labeling. *Neuropsychopharmacology*, 39, 2750-9.

[25] Gross, J.; Lee, J., *et al.* (**1997**). Nicotine-containing versus de-nicotinized cigarettes: effects on craving and withdrawal. *Pharmacol Biochem Behav*, 57, 159-65.

[26] Darredeau, C.; Stewart, S. H., *et al.* (**2013**). The effects of nicotine content information on subjective and behavioural responses to nicotine-containing and denicotinized cigarettes. *Behav Pharmacol*, 24, 291-7.

[27] Hartmann-Boyce, J.; Chepkin, S. C., *et al.* (**2018**). Nicotine replacement therapy versus control for smoking cessation. *Cochrane Database Syst Rev*, 5, CD000146.

[28] Moore, D.; Aveyard, P., *et al.* (**2009**). Effectiveness and safety of nicotine replacement therapy assisted reduction to stop smoking: systematic review and meta-analysis. *BMJ*, 338, b1024.

[29] Etter, J. F. and Stapleton, J. A. (**2006**). Nicotine replacement therapy for long-term smoking cessation: a meta-analysis. *Tob Control*, 15, 280-5.

[30] Hughes, J. R.; Adams, E. H., *et al.* (**2005**). A prospective study of off-label use of, abuse of, and dependence on nicotine inhaler. *Tob Control*, 14, 49-54.

[31] Etter, J. F. (**2007**). Addiction to the nicotine gum in never smokers. *BMC Public Health*, 7, 159.

[32] West, R.; Hajek, P., *et al.* (**2000**). A comparison of the abuse liability and dependence potential of nicotine patch, gum, spray and inhaler. *Psychopharmacology (Berl)*, 149, 198-202.

[33] Dar, R. and Frenk, H. (**2004**). Do smokers self-administer pure nicotine? A review of the evidence. *Psychopharmacology (Berl)*, 173, 18-26.

[34] Garelik, D. A. (**2010**). Nicotine gum dependence treated with varenicline--a case report. *Nicotine Tob Res*, 12, 1041-2.

[35] Mendelsohn, C. P. (**2016**). Three decades of high-dose nicotine gum dependence treated with nicotine patches. *Nicotine Tob Res*, 18, 1220-1.

[36] Hughes, J. R.; Hatsukami, D. K., *et al.* (**1986**). Physical dependence on nicotine in gum. A placebo substitution trial. *JAMA*, 255, 3277-9.

[37] Etter, J. F. and Eissenberg, T. (**2015**). Dependence levels in users of electronic cigarettes, nicotine gums and tobacco cigarettes. *Drug Alcohol Depend*, 147, 68-75.

[38] Schneider, N. G.; Olmstead, R. E., *et al.* (**2001**). The nicotine inhaler: clinical pharmacokinetics and comparison with other nicotine treatments. *Clin Pharmacokinet*, 40, 661-84.

[39] Special Eurobarometer (**2017**). Attitudes of Europeans towards tobacco and electronic cigarettes. https://publications.europa.eu/en/publication-detail/-/publication/c2dc8256-0af0-11e8-966a-01aa75ed71a1/language-en#

[40] U.S. Department of Health and Human Services (**2014**). The health consequences of smoking—50 years of progress: A report of the Surgeon General. https://www.ncbi.nlm.nih.gov/books/NBK179276/pdf/Bookshelf_NBK179276.pdf

[41] Muttarak, R.; Gallus, S., *et al.* (**2013**). Why do smokers start? *Eur J Cancer Prev*, 22, 181-6.

[42] Leonardi-Bee, J.; Jere, M. L., *et al.* (**2011**). Exposure to parental and sibling smoking and the risk of smoking uptake in childhood and adolescence: a systematic review and meta-analysis. *Thorax*, 66, 847-55.

[43] Oh, D. L.; Heck, J. E., *et al.* (**2010**). Determinants of smoking initiation among women in five European countries: a cross-sectional survey. *BMC Public Health*, 10, 74.

[44] Vargas, L. S.; Lucchese, R., *et al.* (**2017**). Determinants of tobacco use by students. *Rev Saude Publica*, 51, 36.

[45] Liu, J.; Zhao, S., *et al.* (**2017**). The influence of peer behavior as a function of social and cultural closeness: A meta-analysis of normative influence on adolescent smoking initiation and continuation. *Psychol Bull*, 143, 1082-115.

[46] World Health Organization, Global Health Observatory Data Repository (**2019**). Smoking prevalence, total (ages 15+). https://data.worldbank.org/indicator/SH.PRV.SMOK

[47] Sheer, V. C.; Mao, C. M., *et al.* (**2017**). Focus group findings of smoking onset among male youth in China. *Subst Use Misuse*, 52, 866-74.

[48] Sheer, V. C. and Mao, C. (**2018**). Cigarette initiation among chinese male teenagers in early smoking interactions. *Health Commun*, 33, 392-400.

[49] World Health Organisation (**2019**). Tobacco factsheet. https://www.who.int/news-room/fact-sheets/detail/tobacco

[50] Casetta, B.; Videla, A. J., *et al.* (**2017**). Association Between Cigarette Smoking Prevalence and Income Level: A Systematic Review and Meta-Analysis. *Nicotine Tob Res*, 19, 1401-7.

[51] Siahpush, M.; Farazi, P. A., *et al.* (**2018**). Socioeconomic status and cigarette expenditure among US households: results from 2010 to 2015 Consumer Expenditure Survey. *BMJ Open*, 8, e020571.

[52] Kennedy, R. D.; Millstein, R. A., *et al.* (**2013**). Tobacco industry strategies to minimize or mask cigarette smoke: opportunities for tobacco product regulation. *Nicotine Tob Res*, 15, 596-602.

[53] Leonardi-Bee, J.; Nderi, M., *et al.* (**2016**). Smoking in movies and smoking initiation in adolescents: systematic review and meta-analysis. *Addiction*, 111, 1750-63.

[54] Murphy, C. M.; Janssen, T., *et al.* (**2019**). Low self-esteem for physical appearance mediates the effect of body mass index on smoking initiation among adolescents. *J Pediatr Psychol*, 44, 197-207.

[55] Pinto Dda, S. and Ribeiro, S. A. (**2007**). Variables related to smoking initiation among students in public and private high schools in the city of Belem, Brazil. *J Bras Pneumol*, 33, 558-64.

[56] Cosh, S.; Hawkins, K., *et al.* (**2015**). Tobacco use among urban Aboriginal Australian young people: a qualitative study of reasons for smoking, barriers to cessation and motivators for smoking cessation. *Aust J Prim Health*, 21, 334-41.

[57] Salvi, D. and Nagarkar, A. (**2018**). A qualitative study exploring women's journeys to becoming smokers in the social context of urban India. *Women Health*, 58, 466-82.

[58] Stubbs, B.; Veronese, N., *et al.* (**2017**). Perceived stress and smoking across 41 countries: A global perspective across Europe, Africa, Asia and the Americas. *Sci Rep*, 7, 7597.

[59] Lawless, M. H.; Harrison, K. A., *et al.* (**2015**). Perceived stress and smoking-related behaviors and symptomatology in male and female smokers. *Addict Behav*, 51, 80-3.

[60] Gallo, L. C.; Roesch, S. C., *et al.* (**2014**). Associations of chronic stress burden, perceived stress, and traumatic stress with cardiovascular disease prevalence and risk factors in the Hispanic Community Health Study/Study of Latinos Sociocultural Ancillary Study. *Psychosom Med*, 76, 468-75.

[61] Webb, M. S. and Carey, M. P. (**2008**). Tobacco smoking among low-income Black women: demographic and psychosocial correlates in a community sample. *Nicotine Tob Res*, 10, 219-29.

[62] Gonzalez, A. M.; Cruz, S. Y., *et al.* (**2013**). Alcohol consumption and smoking and their associations with socio-demographic characteristics, dietary patterns, and perceived academic stress in Puerto Rican college students. *P R Health Sci J*, 32, 82-8.

[63] Cui, X.; Rockett, I. R., *et al.* (**2012**). Work stress, life stress, and smoking among rural-urban migrant workers in China. *BMC Public Health*, 12, 979.

[64] Gruder, C. L.; Trinidad, D. R., *et al.* (**2013**). Tobacco smoking, quitting, and relapsing among adult males in Mainland China: the China Seven Cities Study. *Nicotine Tob Res*, 15, 223-30.

[65] Mead, E. L.; Johnson, S. L., *et al.* (**2018**). Beyond blunts: Reasons for cigarette and cigar use among African American young adult dual users. *Addict Res Theory*, 26, 349–60.

[66] Siddiqui, S. V.; Chatterjee, U., *et al.* (**2008**). Neuropsychology of prefrontal cortex. *Indian J Psychiatry*, 50, 202–8.

[67] Arnsten, A. F. (**2009**). Stress signalling pathways that impair prefrontal cortex structure and function. *Nat Rev Neurosci*, 10, 410–22.

[68] Volman, I.; Roelofs, K., *et al.* (**2011**). Anterior prefrontal cortex inhibition impairs control over social emotional actions. *Curr Biol*, 21, 1766–70.

[69] Goriounova, N. A. and Mansvelder, H. D. (**2012**). Short- and long-term consequences of nicotine exposure during adolescence for prefrontal cortex neuronal network function. *Cold Spring Harb Perspect Med*, 2, a012120.

[70] Bacher, I.; Houle, S., *et al.* (**2011**). Monoamine oxidase A binding in the prefrontal and anterior cingulate cortices during acute withdrawal from heavy cigarette smoking. *Arch Gen Psychiat*, 68, 817–26.

[71] Xu, J.; Mendrek, A., *et al.* (**2007**). Effect of cigarette smoking on prefrontal cortical function in nondeprived smokers performing the Stroop Task. *Neuropsychopharmacology*, 32, 1421–8.

[72] Mansvelder, H. and Goriounova, N. (**2012**). Nicotine exposure during adolescence alters the rules for prefrontal cortical synaptic plasticity during adulthood. *Frontiers in Synaptic Neuroscience*, 4.

[73] Flaudias, V.; Picot, M. C., *et al.* (**2016**). Executive functions in tobacco dependence: Importance of inhibitory capacities. *PLoS One*, 11, e0150940.

[74] Wagner, M.; Schulze-Rauschenbach, S., *et al.* (**2013**). Neurocognitive impairments in non-deprived smokers--results from a population-based multi-center study on smoking-related behavior. *Addict Biol*, 18, 752–61.

[75] Dregan, A.; Stewart, R., *et al.* (**2013**). Cardiovascular risk factors and cognitive decline in adults aged 50 and over: a population-based cohort study. *Age Ageing*, 42, 338–45.

[76] Jansari, A. S.; Froggatt, D., *et al.* (**2013**). Investigating the impact of nicotine on executive functions using a novel virtual reality assessment. *Addiction*, 108, 977–84.

[77] Heffernan, T. M.; Carling, A., *et al.* (**2014**). Smoking impedes executive function and related prospective memory. *Ir J Psychol Med*, 31, 159–65.

[78] Noé-Díaz, V.; Salinas-Rivera, E., *et al.* (**2018**). Changes on executive functions before and after quitting smoking: Pilot study. *Journal of Substance Use*, 23, 452-6.

[79] Nesbitt, P. D. (**1973**). Smoking, physiological arousal, and emotional response. *J Pers Soc Psychol*, 25, 137-44.

[80] Shiffman, S. and Jarvik, M. E. (**1984**). Cigarette smoking, physiological arousal, and emotional response: Nesbitt's paradox re-examined. *Addict Behav*, 9, 95-8.

[81] Pomerleau, C. S. and Pomerleau, O. F. (**1987**). The effects of a psychological stressor on cigarette smoking and subsequent behavioral and physiological responses. *Psychophysiology*, 24, 278-85.

[82] Perkins, K. A.; Grobe, J. E., *et al.* (**1992**). "Paradoxical" effects of smoking on subjective stress versus cardiovascular arousal in males and females. *Pharmacol Biochem Behav*, 42, 301-11.

[83] Parrott, A. C. (**1995**). Stress modulation over the day in cigarette smokers. *Addiction*, 90, 233-44.

[84] Linneberg, A.; Jacobsen, R. K., *et al.* (**2015**). Effect of smoking on blood pressure and resting heart rate: A Mendelian randomization meta-analysis in the CARTA consortium. *Circ Cardiovasc Genet*, 8, 832-41.

[85] Parrott, A. C. (**1998**). Nesbitt's Paradox resolved? Stress and arousal modulation during cigarette smoking. *Addiction*, 93, 27-39.

[86] Wood, W. and Runger, D. (**2016**). Psychology of habit. *Annu Rev Psychol*, 67, 289-314.

[87] Heishman, S. J.; Kleykamp, B. A., *et al.* (**2010**). Meta-analysis of the acute effects of nicotine and smoking on human performance. *Psychopharmacology (Berl)*, 210, 453-69.

[88] Liu, J.-T.; Lee, I. H., *et al.* (**2013**). Cigarette smoking might impair memory and sleep quality. *Journal of the Formosan Medical Association*, 112, 287-90.

[89] Nooyens, A. C. J.; Gelder, B. M. v., *et al.* (**2008**). Smoking and cognitive decline among middle-aged men and women: The Doetinchem cohort study. *American Journal of Public Health*, 98, 2244-50.

[90] Sabia, S.; Marmot, M., *et al.* (**2008**). Smoking history and cognitive function in middle age from the Whitehall II study. *JAMA Internal Medicine*, 168, 1165-73.

[91] Richards, M.; Jarvis, M. J., *et al.* (**2003**). Cigarette smoking and cognitive decline in midlife: evidence from a prospective birth cohort study. *Am J Public Health*, 93, 994-8.

[92] Jacobsen, L. K.; Krystal, J. H., *et al.* (**2005**). Effects of smoking and smoking abstinence on cognition in adolescent tobacco smokers. *Biol Psychiatry*, 57, 56-66.

[93] Ernst, M.; Heishman, S. J., *et al.* (**2001**). Smoking history and nicotine effects on cognitive performance. *Neuropsychopharmacology*, 25, 313-9.

[94] Elwan, O.; Hassan, A. A., *et al.* (**1997**). Brain aging in a sample of normal Egyptians cognition, education, addiction and smoking. *J Neurol Sci*, 148, 79-86.

[95] Yakir, A.; Rigbi, A., *et al.* (**2007**). Why do young women smoke? III. Attention and impulsivity as neurocognitive predisposing factors. *Eur Neuropsychopharmacol*, 17, 339-51.

[96] Fried, P. A.; Watkinson, B., *et al.* (**2006**). Neurocognitive consequences of cigarette smoking in young adults--a comparison with pre-drug performance. *Neurotoxicol Teratol*, 28, 517-25.

[97] Launer, L. J.; Feskens, E. J., *et al.* (**1996**). Smoking, drinking, and thinking. The Zutphen Elderly Study. *Am J Epidemiol*, 143, 219-27.

[98] Zhou, H.; Deng, J., *et al.* (**2003**). Study of the relationship between cigarette smoking, alcohol drinking and cognitive impairment among elderly people in China. *Age Ageing*, 32, 205-10.

[99] Akiyama, H.; Meyer, J. S., *et al.* (**1997**). Normal human aging: factors contributing to cerebral atrophy. *J Neurol Sci*, 152, 39-49.

[100] Kubota, K.; Matsuzawa, T., *et al.* (**1987**). Age-related brain atrophy enhanced by smoking: a quantitative study with computed tomography. *Tohoku J Exp Med*, 153, 303-11.

[101] Hayee, A.; Haque, A., *et al.* (**2003**). Smoking enhances age related brain atrophy--a quantitative study with computed tomography. *Bangladesh Med Res Counc Bull*, 29, 118-24.

[102] Brody, A. L.; Mandelkern, M. A., *et al.* (**2004**). Differences between smokers and nonsmokers in regional gray matter volumes and densities. *Biol Psychiatry*, 55, 77-84.

[103] Almeida, O. P.; Garrido, G. J., *et al.* (**2008**). Smoking is associated with reduced cortical regional gray matter density in brain regions associated with incipient Alzheimer disease. *Am J Geriatr Psychiatry*, 16, 92-8.

[104] Gallinat, J.; Lang, U. E., *et al.* (**2007**). Abnormal hippocampal neurochemistry in smokers: evidence from proton magnetic resonance spectroscopy at 3 T. *J Clin Psychopharmacol*, 27, 80-4.

[105] Gallinat, J.; Meisenzahl, E., *et al.* (**2006**). Smoking and structural brain deficits: a volumetric MR investigation. *Eur J Neurosci*, 24, 1744-50.

[106] Durazzo, T. C.; Meyerhoff, D. J., *et al.* (**2010**). Chronic cigarette smoking: implications for neurocognition and brain neurobiology. *Int J Environ Res Public Health*, 7, 3760-91.

[107] Suwa, K.; Flores, N. M., *et al.* (**2017**). Examining the association of smoking with work productivity and associated costs in Japan. *J Med Econ*, 20, 938-44.

[108] Centers for Disease, C. and Prevention (**2008**). Smoking-attributable mortality, years of potential life lost, and productivity losses--United States, 2000-2004. *MMWR Morb Mortal Wkly Rep*, 57, 1226-8.

[109] Owen, A. J.; Maulida, S. B., *et al.* (**2019**). Productivity burden of smoking in Australia: a life table modelling study. *Tob Control*, 28, 297-304.

[110] Campbell, A. P.; Hoehle, L. P., *et al.* (**2017**). Smoking: An independent risk factor for lost productivity in chronic rhinosinusitis. *Laryngoscope*, 127, 1742-5.

[111] Baker, C. L.; Flores, N. M., *et al.* (**2017**). Benefits of quitting smoking on work productivity and activity impairment in the United States, the European Union and China. *Int J Clin Pract*, 71.

[112] Conway, T. L. (**1998**). Tobacco use and the United States military: a longstanding problem. *Tob Control*, 7, 219-21.

[113] Talcott, G. W.; Ebbert, J. O., *et al.* (**2015**). Tobacco research in the military: Reflections on 20 years of research in the United States Air Force. *Mil Med*, 180, 848-50.

[114] Smith, E. A.; Poston, W. S., *et al.* (**2016**). Installation tobacco control programs in the U.S. Military. *Mil Med*, 181, 596-601.

[115] Bedno, S. A.; Jackson, R., *et al.* (**2017**). Meta-analysis of cigarette smoking and musculoskeletal injuries in military training. *Med Sci Sports Exerc*, 49, 2191-7.

[116] Le Foll, B.; Guranda, M., *et al.* (**2014**). Elevation of dopamine induced by cigarette smoking: novel insights from a [11C]-+-PHNO PET study in humans. *Neuropsychopharmacology*, 39, 415-24.

[117] Wing, V. C.; Payer, D. E., *et al.* (**2015**). Measuring cigarette smoking-induced cortical dopamine release: A [(1)(1)C]FLB-457 PET study. *Neuropsychopharmacology*, 40, 1417-27.

[118] In: Lynch BS, Bonnie RJ, editors. Growing up tobacco free: Preventing nicotine addiction in children and youths. Washington (DC): Institute of Medicine (US) Committee on Preventing Nicotine Addiction in Children and Youths; **1994**. https://www.ncbi.nlm.nih.gov/pubmed/25144107

[119] Ashok, A. H.; Mizuno, Y., *et al.* (**2019**). Tobacco smoking and dopaminergic function in humans: a meta-analysis of molecular imaging studies. *Psychopharmacology (Berl)*, 236, 1119-29.

[120] Hogg, R. C. (**2016**). Contribution of monoamine oxidase inhibition to tobacco dependence: A review of the evidence. *Nicotine Tob Res*, 18, 509-23.

[121] Lewis, A.; Miller, J. H., *et al.* (**2007**). Monoamine oxidase and tobacco dependence. *Neurotoxicology*, 28, 182-95.

[122] Gilbert, D. G.; Zuo, Y., *et al.* (**2003**). Platelet monoamine oxidase B activity changes across 31 days of smoking abstinence. *Nicotine Tob Res*, 5, 813-9.

[123] Smith, K. S. and Graybiel, A. M. (**2016**). Habit formation. *Dialogues Clin Neurosci*, 18, 33-43.

[124] Wang, L. P.; Li, F., *et al.* (**2011**). NMDA receptors in dopaminergic neurons are crucial for habit learning. *Neuron*, 72, 1055-66.

[125] Wickens, J. R.; Horvitz, J. C., *et al.* (**2007**). Dopaminergic mechanisms in actions and habits. *J Neurosci*, 27, 8181-3.

[126] Horsfall, L. (**2016**). The nocebo effect. *SAAD Dig*, 32, 55-7.

[127] Hakulinen, C.; Hintsanen, M., *et al.* (**2015**). Personality and smoking: individual-participant meta-analysis of nine cohort studies. *Addiction*, 110, 1844-52.

[128] McCrae, R. R.; Martin, T. A., *et al.* (**2005**). Age trends and age norms for the NEO Personality Inventory-3 in adolescents and adults. *Assessment*, 12, 363-73.

[129] Prochaska, J. and Diclemente, C. (**1982**). Trans-theoretical therapy - toward a more integrative model of change. *Psychotherapy: Theory, Research & Practice*, 19, 276-88.

[130] Prochaska, J. O. and DiClemente, C. C. (**1983**). Stages and processes of self-change of smoking: toward an integrative model of change. *J Consult Clin Psychol*, 51, 390-5.

[131] Joly, B.; Perriot, J., *et al.* (**2017**). Success rates in smoking cessation: Psychological preparation plays a critical role and interacts with other factors such as psychoactive substances. *PLoS One*, 12, e0184800.

[132] Larabie, L. C. (**2005**). To what extent do smokers plan quit attempts? *Tob Control*, 14, 425-8.

[133] Martijn, C.; Tenbült, P., *et al.* (**2002**). Getting A Grip on Ourselves: Challenging Expectancies About Loss of Energy After Self-Control. *Social Cognition*, 20, 441-60.

[134] Inzlicht, M. and Gutsell, J. N. (**2007**). Running on empty: neural signals for self-control failure. *Psychol Sci*, 18, 933-7.

[135] Ward, T. (**2001**). Using psychological insights to help people quit smoking. *J Adv Nurs*, 34, 754-9.

[136] Cooper, S.; Orton, S., *et al.* (**2017**). Smoking and quit attempts during pregnancy and postpartum: a longitudinal UK cohort. *BMJ Open*, 7, e018746.

[137] Lange, S.; Probst, C., *et al.* (**2018**). National, regional, and global prevalence of smoking during pregnancy in the general population: a systematic review and meta-analysis. *Lancet Glob Health*, 6, e769-e76.

[138] Riaz, M.; Lewis, S., *et al.* (**2018**). Predictors of smoking cessation during pregnancy: a systematic review and meta-analysis. *Addiction*, 113, 610-22.

[139] Colman, G. J. and Joyce, T. (**2003**). Trends in smoking before, during, and after pregnancy in ten states. *Am J Prev Med*, 24, 29-35.

[140] Letourneau, A. R.; Sonja, B., *et al.* (**2007**). Timing and predictors of postpartum return to smoking in a group of inner-city women: an exploratory pilot study. *Birth*, 34, 245-52.

[141] Gallus, S.; Muttarak, R., *et al.* (**2013**). Why do smokers quit? *Eur J Cancer Prev*, 22, 96-101.

[142] Sieminska, A.; Buczkowski, K., *et al.* (**2008**). Patterns of motivations and ways of quitting smoking among Polish smokers: a questionnaire study. *BMC Public Health*, 8, 274.

[143] Banderali, G.; Martelli, A., *et al.* (**2015**). Short and long term health effects of parental tobacco smoking during pregnancy and lactation: a descriptive review. *J Transl Med*, 13, 327.

[144] Beal, M. A.; Yauk, C. L., *et al.* (**2017**). From sperm to offspring: Assessing the heritable genetic consequences of paternal smoking and potential public health impacts. *Mutat Res*, 773, 26-50.

[145] Tinuoye, O.; Pell, J. P., *et al.* (**2013**). Meta-analysis of the association between secondhand smoke exposure and physician-diagnosed childhood asthma. *Nicotine Tob Res*, 15, 1475-83.

[146] Hur, K.; Liang, J., *et al.* (**2014**). The role of secondhand smoke in allergic rhinitis: a systematic review. *Int Forum Allergy Rhinol*, 4, 110-6.

[147] Zhou, S.; Rosenthal, D. G., *et al.* (**2014**). Physical, behavioral, and cognitive effects of prenatal tobacco and postnatal secondhand smoke exposure. *Curr Probl Pediatr Adolesc Health Care*, 44, 219-41.

[148] Samet, J. M. (**2019**). Secondhand smoke exposure: Effects in adults. *UpToDate*, https://www.uptodate.com/contents/secondhand-smoke-exposure-effects-in-adults.

[149] Mucha, L.; Stephenson, J., *et al.* (**2006**). Meta-analysis of disease risk associated with smoking, by gender and intensity of smoking. *Gend Med*, 3, 279-91.

[150] Saha, S. P.; Bhalla, D. K., *et al.* (**2007**). Cigarette smoke and adverse health effects: An overview of research trends and future needs. *Int J Angiol*, 16, 77-83.

[151] Centers for disease control and prevention (**2019**). Health effects of cigarette smoking. https://www.cdc.gov/tobacco/data_statistics/fact_sheets/health_effects/effects_cig_smoking/index.htm

[152] Baumeister, R. F.; Bratslavsky, E., *et al.* (**1998**). Ego depletion: is the active self a limited resource? *J Pers Soc Psychol*, 74, 1252-65.

[153] Arber, M. M.; Ireland, M. J., *et al.* (**2017**). Ego depletion in real-time: An examination of the sequential-task paradigm. *Front Psychol*, 8, 1672.

[154] Vohs, K. D. and Heatherton, T. F. (**2000**). Self-regulatory failure: a resource-depletion approach. *Psychol Sci*, 11, 249-54.

[155] Job, V.; Dweck, C. S., *et al.* (**2010**). Ego depletion--is it all in your head? implicit theories about willpower affect self-regulation. *Psychol Sci*, 21, 1686-93.

[156] Webb, T. L. and Sheeran, P. (**2003**). Can implementation intentions help to overcome ego-depletion? *J Exp Soc Psychol*, 39, 279-86.

[157] Muraven, M. and Baumeister, R. F. (**2000**). Self-regulation and depletion of limited resources: does self-control resemble a muscle? *Psychol Bull*, 126, 247-59.

[158] Muraven, M.; Baumeister, R. F., *et al.* (**1999**). Longitudinal improvement of self-regulation through practice: building self-control strength through repeated exercise. *J Soc Psychol*, 139, 446-57.

[159] Muraven, M. (**2010**). Practicing self-control lowers the risk of smoking lapse. *Psychol Addict Behav*, 24, 446-52.

[160] Oaten, M. and Cheng, K. (**2006**). Improved self-control: The benefits of a regular program of academic study. *Basic and Applied Social Psychology*, 28, 1-16.

[161] Baumeister, R. F.; Gailliot, M., *et al.* (**2006**). Self-regulation and personality: how interventions increase regulatory success, and how depletion moderates the effects of traits on behavior. *J Pers*, 74, 1773-801.

[162] Gailliot, M. T.; Baumeister, R. F., *et al.* (**2007**). Self-control relies on glucose as a limited energy source: willpower is more than a metaphor. *J Pers Soc Psychol*, 92, 325-36.

[163] Chaput, J. P. and Tremblay, A. (**2009**). The glucostatic theory of appetite control and the risk of obesity and diabetes. *Int J Obes (Lond)*, 33, 46-53.

[164] Treloar, H. R.; Piasecki, T. M., *et al.* (**2014**). Relations among caffeine consumption, smoking, smoking urge, and subjective smoking reinforcement in daily life. *J Caffeine Res*, 4, 93-9.

[165] Treur, J. L.; Taylor, A. E., *et al.* (**2016**). Associations between smoking and caffeine consumption in two European cohorts. *Addiction*, 111, 1059-68.

[166] Brewer, J. A.; Mallik, S., *et al.* (**2011**). Mindfulness training for smoking cessation: results from a randomized controlled trial. *Drug Alcohol Depend*, 119, 72-80.

[167] Sun, X.; Prochaska, J. O., *et al.* (**2007**). Transtheoretical principles and processes for quitting smoking: a 24-month comparison of a representative sample of quitters, relapsers, and non-quitters. *Addict Behav*, 32, 2707-26.

[168] Oaten, M. and Cheng, K. (**2006**). Longitudinal gains in self-regulation from regular physical exercise. *Br J Health Psychol*, 11, 717-33.

[169] Yue, G. and Cole, K. J. (**1992**). Strength increases from the motor program: comparison of training with maximal voluntary and imagined muscle contractions. *J Neurophysiol*, 67, 1114-23.

[170] Ranganathan, V. K.; Siemionow, V., *et al.* (**2004**). From mental power to muscle power--gaining strength by using the mind. *Neuropsychologia*, 42, 944-56.

[171] Pascual-Leone, A.; Nguyet, D., *et al.* (**1995**). Modulation of muscle responses evoked by transcranial magnetic stimulation during the acquisition of new fine motor skills. *J Neurophysiol*, 74, 1037-45.

[172] Palmiero, M.; Nori, R., *et al.* (**2015**). Domain-Specificity of Creativity: A Study on the Relationship Between Visual Creativity and Visual Mental Imagery. *Front Psychol*, 6, 1870.

[173] Garcia Carrasco, D. and Aboitiz Cantalapiedra, J. (**2016**). Effectiveness of motor imagery or mental practice in functional recovery after stroke: a systematic review. *Neurologia*, 31, 43-52.

[174] Braun, S.; Kleynen, M., *et al.* (**2008**). Using mental practice in stroke rehabilitation: a framework. *Clin Rehabil*, 22, 579-91.

[175] Kho, A. Y.; Liu, K. P., *et al.* (**2014**). Meta-analysis on the effect of mental imagery on motor recovery of the hemiplegic upper extremity function. *Aust Occup Ther J*, 61, 38-48.

[176] Butler, A. J. and Page, S. J. (**2006**). Mental practice with motor imagery: evidence for motor recovery and cortical reorganization after stroke. *Arch Phys Med Rehabil*, 87, S2-11.

[177] Yeomans, K.; Payne, K. A., *et al.* (**2011**). Smoking, smoking cessation and smoking relapse patterns: a web-based survey of current and former smokers in the US. *Int J Clin Pract*, 65, 1043-54.

[178] Cheong, Y.; Yong, H. H., *et al.* (**2007**). Does how you quit affect success? A comparison between abrupt and gradual methods using data from the International Tobacco Control Policy Evaluation Study. *Nicotine Tob Res*, 9, 801-10.

[179] Doran, C. M.; Valenti, L., *et al.* (**2006**). Smoking status of Australian general practice patients and their attempts to quit. *Addict Behav*, 31, 758-66.

[180] Lindson-Hawley, N.; Banting, M., *et al.* (**2016**). Gradual versus abrupt smoking cessation: A randomized, controlled noninferiority trial. *Ann Intern Med*, 164, 585-92.

[181] Fagerstrom, K. O. (**2005**). Can reduced smoking be a way for smokers not interested in quitting to actually quit? *Respiration*, 72, 216-20.

[182] Tan, J.; Zhao, L., *et al.* (**2019**). A meta-analysis of the effectiveness of gradual versus abrupt smoking cessation. *Tob Induc Dis*, 17, 1-6.

[183] U.S. Department of Health and Human Services (**2008**). Treating tobacco use and dependence: 2008 update. http://www.tobaccoprogram.org/clientuploads/documents/Consumer%20 Materials/Clinicians%20Systems%20Mat/2008-Guidelines.pdf

[184] Hughes, J. R. and Klemperer, E. M. (**2016**). Gradual versus abrupt smoking cessation. *Ann Intern Med*, 165, 741.

[185] Khariwala, S. S.; Rubin, N., *et al.* (**2019**). "Cold turkey" or pharmacotherapy: Examination of tobacco cessation methods tried among smokers prior to developing head and neck cancer. *Head Neck*, 41, 2332-9.

[186] Haug, S.; Schaub, M. P., *et al.* (**2014**). Predictors of adolescent smoking cessation and smoking reduction. *Patient Educ Couns*, 95, 378-83.

[187] Muraven, M. and Slessareva, E. (**2003**). Mechanisms of self-control failure: motivation and limited resources. *Pers Soc Psychol Bull*, 29, 894-906.

[188] Muraven, M. (**2008**). Autonomous self-control is less depleting. *J Res Pers*, 42, 763-70.

[189] Schuurmans, M. M. (**2016**). Gradual versus abrupt smoking cessation. *Ann Intern Med*, 165, 741-2.

[190] Hughes, J. R.; Dash, M., *et al.* (**2015**). Is impulsivity a symptom of initial tobacco withdrawal? A meta-analysis and qualitative systematic review. *Nicotine Tob Res*, 17, 503-9.

[191] McLaughlin, I.; Dani, J. A., *et al.* (**2015**). Nicotine withdrawal. *Curr Top Behav Neurosci*, 24, 99-123.

[192] Taylor, G.; McNeill, A., *et al.* (**2014**). Change in mental health after smoking cessation: systematic review and meta-analysis. *BMJ*, 348, g1151.

[193] Kim, S. J.; Chae, W., *et al.* (**2019**). The impact of smoking cessation attempts on stress levels. *BMC Public Health*, 19, 267.

[194] Zarghami, M.; Taghizadeh, F., *et al.* (**2018**). Efficacy of smoking cessation on stress, anxiety, and depression in smokers with chronic obstructive pulmonary disease: A randomized controlled clinical trial. *Addict Health*, 10, 137-47.

[195] Brose, L. S.; Simonavicius, E., *et al.* (**2018**). Maintaining abstinence from smoking after a period of enforced abstinence - systematic review, meta-analysis and analysis of behaviour change techniques with a focus on mental health. *Psychol Med*, 48, 669-78.

[196] Aubin, H. J.; Farley, A., *et al.* (**2012**). Weight gain in smokers after quitting cigarettes: meta-analysis. *BMJ*, 345, e4439.

[197] Tian, J.; Venn, A., *et al.* (**2015**). The association between quitting smoking and weight gain: a systematic review and meta-analysis of prospective cohort studies. *Obes Rev*, 16, 883-901.

[198] Harris, K. K.; Zopey, M., *et al.* (**2016**). Metabolic effects of smoking cessation. *Nat Rev Endocrinol*, 12, 299-308.

[199] Pavlidis, P.; Gouveris, H., *et al.* (**2017**). Electrogustometry Thresholds, Tongue Tip Vascularization, Density, and Form of the Fungiform Papillae Following Smoking Cessation. *Chem Senses*, 42, 419–23.

[200] Pavlidis, P.; Gouveris, C., *et al.* (**2014**). Changes in electrogustometry thresholds, tongue tip vascularization, density and form of the fungiform papillae in smokers. *Eur Arch Otorhinolaryngol*, 271, 2325–31.

[201] Cheruel, F.; Jarlier, M., *et al.* (**2017**). Effect of cigarette smoke on gustatory sensitivity, evaluation of the deficit and of the recovery time-course after smoking cessation. *Tob Induc Dis*, 15, 15.

[202] Chambers, L.; McCrickerd, K., *et al.* (**2015**). Optimising foods for satiety. *Trends in Food Science & Technology*, 41, 149–60.

[203] Geha, P. Y.; Aschenbrenner, K., *et al.* (**2013**). Altered hypothalamic response to food in smokers. *Am J Clin Nutr*, 97, 15–22.

[204] Benton, D. and Young, H. A. (**2015**). Do small differences in hydration status affect mood and mental performance? *Nutr Rev*, 73 Suppl 2, 83–96.

www.ingramcontent.com/pod-product-compliance
Lightning Source LLC
Chambersburg PA
CBHW031108250726
48655CB00004B/1633